A CÉZANNE IN THE HEDGE

and other memories of Charleston and Bloomsbury

A CÉZANNE IN THE HEDGE

and other memories of Charleston and Bloomsbury

FOREWORD BY

MICHAEL HOLROYD

EDITED BY

HUGH LEE

C&B
COLLINS & BROWN

First published in Great Britain in 1992 by
COLLINS & BROWN LIMITED
Mercury House
195 Knightsbridge
London SW7 1RE

British Library Cataloguing-in-Publication Data:
A catalogue record for this book is available from the British Library.

ISBN 1 85585 104 0 (hardback edition)
ISBN 1 85585 121 0 (paperback edition)

Designed by Peter Bridgewater
Typeset by Falcon Graphic Art,
Wallington, Surrey
Printed and bound in Great Britain by
The Bath Press

CONTENTS

FOREWORD

Michael Holroyd

When I signed the contract for my Life of Lytton Strachey in the early 1960s, I was given by way of advance the sum of fifty pounds. At that time I had written only an as yet unpublished study of a little known and impoverished man of letters, Hugh Kingsmill. So this contract, which recalled to my mind an observation made by Kingsmill about one of his own advances (that it looked 'more like a retreat than an advance') accurately reflected my lack of status as a biographer. But it was also, I believe, some measurement of where the Bloomsbury group stood in what Noël Annan calls 'the stock exchange of culture'. In 1960 Strachey's books were not available in paperback and Virginia Woolf was not yet the feminist inspiration she was to become after the rise of feminist criticism in the late 1960s. The reputation of E.M. Forster seemed in decline. The paintings of Duncan Grant and Vanessa Bell were not much privately collected and had sunk into the cellars of many public galleries. The art criticism of Roger Fry and Clive Bell was no longer considered to be of much significance, and almost no one knew the name of Carrington. The best known member of the group was probably Maynard Keynes – the man who stepped into the political world and guarded Bloomsbury's interests while great changes were erupting in the twentieth century. It appeared that he had not done a good job.

A few months before I presented my cheque for fifty pounds to my bank, the first volume of Leonard Woolf's autobiography, entitled *Sowing*, was published. It covered his own origins and early years, as well as the origins of the Bloomsbury group at Cambridge within that famously secret society known as the Apostles. Though none of us knew it then, Bloomsbury was soon to have its revival. Towards the end of the 1950s we had been told by Harold Macmillan that we had never had it so good. After almost two decades of austerity we were about to enter the land of plenty. There could have been no better Bloomsbury ambassador to lead us from the 1950s into the 1960s than Leonard Woolf. As well as being an original member of the group he was also a prominent member of the Fabian Society. The Fabians had seen many of their articles of faith enacted with the rise of socialism, the creation of the National Health Service and the expansion of the Welfare State in the 1940s and early 1950s. But the 'swinging Sixties', which were to witness legislation of the Wolfenden Report recommendations on homosexuality, belonged to Bloomsbury. By the time Leonard Woolf's fifth and last volume of autobiography appeared in 1969, the renewal of interest in Bloomsbury was fully under way.

The Fabians had believed that progress to a better life depended upon a more equal distribution of wealth and the abolition of the British class system. Bloomsbury gave priority to civilized private values over the vulgar ambitions of public life and believed that the good life was made up of aesthetic sensibility and personal relationships. The members of Bloomsbury were artists, the Fabians were sociologists. Bloomsbury was individualistic, the Fabians were collectivists. Bloomsbury chose G.E. Moore and Sigmund Freud as its gurus; the Fabians chose Bernard Shaw and Karl Marx. Searching for a new way in which to judge conduct, Noël Annan said in a celebrated broadcast that the 1920s had come to see the world through the eyes of either Beatrice Webb or Virginia Woolf.

In his contribution to this anthology, John Russell remarks on the contrast between Charleston and Bernard Shaw's house at Ayot St Lawrence. There could be no more vivid way of seeing the differing Fabian and Bloomsbury cultures. In the aftermath of Darwinism many people had transferred their service to God into a duty to the community, and Fabianism had flourished on a new wave of social progressiveness. It seems fitting that 'Shaw's Corner' as it became known was a late Victorian rectory. It was a plain, dark red villa, standing in two acres of sloping ground in a twelfth-century agricultural village where, according to Shaw himself, the last thing of importance that had happened was probably the Flood. Shaw and his wife Charlotte moved there in 1906. Neither of them liked it much and they did not intend to remain there long. But it proved so useful, neither obstructing

Charlotte's love of foreign travel nor distracting GBS's passion for work, that they stayed on until their deaths some forty years later. As a good socialist, Shaw was to nationalize his house by presenting it before his death to the National Trust. To prepare for this he moved down many of his possessions so that, though not looking exactly as it did when he was there, the house bristled with authentic Shaviana. Here are his alphabetical and vegetarian postcards, old typewriter and weighing scales, the photographs of Ibsen and William Morris, Gandhi and Stalin. Shaw excelled at the art in which Bloomsbury was deficient: music. But there is little evidence of this except for the scores that were sent to him and an ancient wireless set. There *are* works of art in the house: but they are almost all likenesses of GBS, from the doorknob on the front door to the Rodin bust and Augustus John portrait inside. At the end of the garden, in what you may easily mistake for a toolshed, is the revolving hut where he worked austerely on world problems out of the world's reach. In this meagre hut he was surrounded by all the innocent technology of his trade – thermometer, alarm clock, chair and bunk. It is touching, almost heartbreaking, evidence of the Fabian work ethic.

There was no such asceticism at Charleston. Going there is still like stepping into and becoming part of a Bloomsbury picture – perhaps indeed it is the masterpiece of Duncan Grant and Vanessa Bell. Urged on by Leonard and Virginia Woolf ('It is very exciting to think that you may get Charleston', Virginia wrote to her sister), the two painters had moved in, together with Clive Bell, late in 1916, and soon filled the ramshackle farmhouse with ceaseless activity, all sorts of aesthetic projects and what Virginia Woolf called the 'whole atmosphere of ragamuffin delight'. In a letter to Roger Fry, Vanessa wrote: 'it's most lovely, very solid and simple, with flat walls in that lovely mixture of brick and flint that they use about here and perfectly flat windows in the walls and wonderfully tiled roofs. The pond is most beautiful with a willow at one side and a stone or flint wall edging it all round the garden part, and a little lawn sloping down to it with formal bushes in it. Then there's a small orchard and walled garden and another lawn and bit of field railed in beyond . . . Inside the house the rooms are very large and a great many . . . but it's nice to have space and no doubt it will get filled in time . . . It will be an odd life . . .

but it seems to me it ought to be a good one for painting.'

Charleston soon became a place of family parties, summer picnics, amateur plays; a place for work and walks by day, late night gossiping and listening to gramophone records. The household was divided between the studio and the study. While Duncan and Vanessa painted, and were occasionally visited by other painters – Roger Fry or Janie Bussy – Clive wrote his books and articles for the *New Statesman*. Many of those who came to stay were writers. David Garnett had moved in at the beginning so that, as a conscientious objector, he could do 'work of national importance' on the farm nearby. After resigning from the Treasury, Maynard Keynes spent the summer of 1919 writing *The Economic Consequences of the Peace* there. 'Nessa presides over the most astonishing *ménage*,' Virginia Woolf wrote that year; 'Belgian hares, governesses, children, gardeners, hens, ducks, and painting all the time, till every inch of the house is a different colour.'

Twelve years later, visiting the house in January 1931, Virginia Woolf likened it to a 'red cave in the profound winter hollow'. But it was in the summer months that it became a specially enchanted place. Frances Partridge remembers it for its strong warm personality. It was a 'place of such potent individuality,' she wrote in her *Memoirs*, 'that whenever I stayed there I came away grateful to it, as it were, for giving me so much pleasure, so many rich and various visual sensations, such talk, such a sense that lives were being intensely and purposely led there . . . I tend to picture it at noon on a summer day, with the tall flowers motionless in the hot still air, their corollas buzzing with bees; a dragon-fly or two skimming over the duckweed-covered pond; and a small group sitting outside the drawing-room French windows in those indestructible but inelegant canvas chairs . . . The house gave the impression of having developed spontaneously, like some vigorous vegetable growth, in spite of the display of human creative energy that covered the walls of all its rooms; for Duncan and Vanessa couldn't see an empty flat space without wanting to cover it with flowers and nudes, with vases and swirls . . . '

Charleston enjoyed its heyday during the 1920s and 1930s. Growing up there, Angelica Garnett remembers, felt like being 'bathed in the glow of perpetual summer'. But the atmosphere was sometimes curiously charged in the aftermath of past emotional storms, still affected by the conflicting pressure and intensity of lives 'purposely led'.

By the time I visited Charleston one autumn in the mid-1960s it wore the air of a Sleeping Beauty. As Lytton Strachey's biographer, I had come to see Duncan Grant during his last rather solitary period there. Perhaps because I felt rather apprehensive, I was not particularly observant that day and can remember few details clearly. There were good reasons for my nervousness. Unknown to Duncan I possessed copies of his correspondence with Strachey which was to form one of my chief sources for Strachey's early life. Put yourself in his place. He was then eighty and confronted by a stranger half-a-century younger than himself who was proposing to make public details of his unorthodox sexual and emotional life in the first decade of the century. It was a testing moment for us both.

Duncan was celebrated for his charm and I fell easily under its spell. He took me round the house and showed me the pictures in all the rooms. Stopping before one of them he explained that it was an early Vanessa Bell. 'Or is it one of mine?', he hazarded. We shook our heads and moved on. I was aware of an amiable conglomeration of good-looking objects everywhere. The sun shone and we walked in the garden. At lunch we ate off Bloomsberry plates and afterwards sat beside the decorated fireplace. What I chiefly noticed about Duncan's conversation was its deceptive simplicity. He would say something – perhaps in answer to one of my biographer's questions – and since what he said sounded simple I would immediately accept it at face value. But a few minutes later I would become aware of a second possible meaning and could not tell whether this had been intended. Duncan was a master of these beguiling *double entendres*.

My day at Charleston taught me something about Bloomsbury that I could never have picked up so vividly from academic research alone. It was here that Lytton Strachey had read out his *Eminent Victorians* to Clive and Vanessa Bell, David Garnett and Duncan Grant (who fell asleep). Those who believe that Bloomsbury was a society of reciprocal civilities should examine the reactions of Strachey's friends to this first performance of his work. Only David Garnett was truly enthusiastic. What was also important, I believe, underlying Bloomsbury's private values as opposed to the more public concerns of the Fabians, was Strachey's decision to make his first audience this private group of friends.

Duncan Grant could not have exemplified the virtues of Bloomsbury more generously. He gave me a drawing for the jacket of my book, allowed me to use his letters, wrote to me giving his early memories of Strachey, and made 'his own contribution to the emancipated climate of the Sixties,' the art historian Richard Shone later wrote, 'just as he had participated in a similar movement half a century before'. Let those who feel tempted to dismiss the Bloomsbury group as a timid self-regarding coterie ask themselves whether, had their own principles come to be tested in such an awkward practical fashion, they would have passed the test with such style and courage.

INTRODUCTION

BLOOMSBURY'S UPS AND DOWNS

Noël Annan

I HAVE BEEN asked to assess Bloomsbury's reputation over the years; and since we live in times where the entrepreneur has become the national ideal, I search for an appropriate metaphor. On the stock exchange of culture, the market in Bloomsburys has always been volatile, partly because the performance of its subsidiary companies has been erratic. Stracheys reached a high between the two Wars, but suffered a catastrophic decline in the Fifties and Sixties and have never totally recovered their one time value despite a rally on Wall Street this year. On the other hand Forsters proved to be remarkably firm right up to the Eighties, though they have eased somewhat since then. Woolfs were bought by discerning investors in the Twenties but it was not until the company diversified with the publication of the biography, diaries and letters that the stock went through the roof. Keynes was for years considered a blue chip share, such was the enormous investment made in this company after the War; but in the Eighties some heavy selling developed and the market has still not settled. The Corporate Group survived a concentrated attack by a firm of predators trading under the name of Leavis, and the value of the shares fell considerably. But by the Eighties Leavis had gone bankrupt and Bloomsburys made a good recovery. In the long-term future investors can be confident that there will be a modest but secure return on their investment.

The truth, of course, is that Bloomsbury has always aroused strong opposition; and the opposition comes from a number of quarters. From the start the *bien pensants* were disgusted. Victorians such as G.M. Young (whose *Portrait of an Age* is still the best short account of Victorian Britain) were outraged by *Eminent Victorians*. 'We are in for a bad time', he said as he laid down the book. Young did not understand that both Strachey and Keynes were writing polemics. Keynes's polemic against Versailles was born from contempt for the folly of governments and the venality of their leaders – leaders who had not the courage to ignore the evil hatreds that the War had unleashed. They should have persuaded their countrymen to see that a just peace based on reason would also be a prosperous peace. Strachey's polemic was against the Victorian establishment and its culture. For was it not that culture which condoned, and even glorified, the terrible slaughter of the Great War? The essay on Gordon attacked imperialism, power politics and evangelical Christianity; the essay on Arnold the public school ethos that turned out the Christian gentleman who fought unthinkingly in that war; the essay on Manning the worldly-wise deviousness of the Church of Rome; and the essay on Florence Nightingale the humanitarianism with which Victorians salved their conscience. Strachey replaced the portrait of the Lady with the Lamp with the picture of a ruthless bird of prey destroying anyone who stood in her way – not a swan but an eagle.

So between the Wars generals, headmasters, archbishops and the like were unlikely to warm to Bloomsbury. Nor were politicians. Bloomsbury regarded worldly success as a deviation from the things in life that mattered and likely to corrupt. But then, strangely enough, neither were they all that popular with the *avant-garde*. Bloomsbury was indeed part of that artistic revolution, Modernism, under whose shadow we still live: the painting of Picasso and Matisse, the experimental novel, the revolution of psychoanalysis and analytic philosophy. The championing of the Post-Impressionists by Roger Fry and Clive Bell was not forgotten; but the German Expressionists passed them by; and so too the Surrealists. In literature their praise of Eliot and their support of D.H. Lawrence was also not forgotten. But Eliot distanced himself gently but decidedly from them after his conversion to Anglicanism; and Lawrence broke with them. Virginia Woolf and Strachey both detested Joyce. Forster, Leonard Woolf and Keynes looked indulgently upon the passion with which the younger generation opposed Fascism. But none of them had any sympathy for Communism, and Forster gently reproved Julian Bell for letting his heart rule his head. He did, however, always retain the affection of Auden and Isherwood, all the more so when, converted to pacifism, they went to America and stayed there during the War; and he ticked off Harold Nicolson and others for lampooning them.

There was another set between the Wars that spoke of them

with marked reservation. They were the Oxford wits. The wits might visit Garsington but they passed by Bloomsbury. They thought its inhabitants dowdy, middle class, lacking in vitality and insufficiently cosmopolitan and modernist. Anthony Powell considered Virginia Woolf inferior to Ivy Compton Burnett. They regarded Forster as an old maid and a pious moralist. Bloomsbury ventured into the fashionable world and withdrew. The Oxford wits took it as a world to conquer. Harold Acton, Evelyn Waugh, Cyril Connolly and the rest lived for pleasure; Forster said Connolly gave pleasure a bad name. They were undismayed by the charge of snobbery and they were animated by competitiveness, impressed, as Connolly said, 'by money and titles and the necessity of coming into close contact with them'. If they looked up to any among their seniors, it was to the Sitwells. In art they were less severe. Compare Kenneth Clark as a critic with Roger Fry: Clark's first significant work was on the Gothic revival and he was later to praise John Betjeman for rescuing the Victorian arts from obloquy. Nor did the successors to the wits at Oxford find Bloomsbury to their taste. Isaiah Berlin referred to the chamber music of Bloomsbury and Goronwy Rees, Stuart Hampshire or Norman O. Brown had scarcely a word to say for them. Only Stephen Spender warmed to Virginia Woolf.

But Bloomsbury had even more formidable enemies. These were the dons. Bloomsbury had no love for academics. Strachey insinuated that the worst enemies of literature were the professors who spent years trying to prove Racine inferior to Shakespeare or, more likely, taking refuge in philology and prosody to avoid discussing why poetry moved men and women.

The historians detested Strachey and, between the Wars, watched with dismay his influence upon clever entrants for the scholarship exams at Oxford and Cambridge. One of them, an eccentric clergyman at Trinity, finally convicted Strachey of deliberately manufacturing a falsehood about Manning (though to this charge Michael Holroyd constructed an ingenious defence). Similarly orthodox economists were indignant that Keynes exaggerated in the *General Theory* (as they thought) his differences from Alfred Marshall.

And then, as if to meet Strachey's challenge, Cambridge set up a faculty of English that did not compel students to learn Anglo-Saxon and study genres and influences. The dons were determined to meet Bloomsbury's criticisms and some of the younger lecturers, such as F.L. Lucas and George Rylands, were second generation Bloomsberries. Most agreed with Bloomsbury that to explain what a writer was at, what he was saying, came first and judgement a long way second. But in 1920 Eliot published *The Sacred Wood* and two years later I.A. Richards published the first of his works on criticism. Eliot pontificated from a great height, but Richards invented a new critical method. He asked his class the author, date and meaning of the poems he handed to them. But he also asked why they thought one poem better than another. Once you asked that question it was inevitable that someone would set out what criteria you had for saying so. Frank and Queenie Leavis did that.

Leavis's criticism rested on an analysis of English culture. The ethos of Bloomsbury, he said, had debased high culture. They had turned it into coterie culture. Bloomsbury's coterie set a vulgar elegance above sincerity. They established a court of cosy self-flatterers. They adopted as their own the limited, if disinterested, philosophy of G.E. Moore and turned his austere method into the dialectic of a coterie. This dialectic, the product of their immature undergraduate days, they then used complacently for the rest of their lives. They claimed to be unworldly but they were in fact merely setters of fashion. It was no excuse to argue that the money Keynes amassed by speculation was spent on learning and the arts: he was corrupted by the act of amassing it. Bloomsbury substituted social-personal values for real values. It created a network of on-the-make dons, literary editors who controlled government agencies and *chic* journals, and who joined with the vulgarians and showmen in ignoring the awkward spiky geniuses of our time such as Lawrence. How was it possible that the high seriousness of Henry Sidgwick and Leslie Stephen had been replaced at Cambridge by Russell's brittle intellect, Forster's feeble Hellenism and Lytton Strachey's sneer? Leavis indicted Bloomsbury in a memorable sentence. 'Articulateness and unreality cultivated together, callowness disguising itself in articulateness; conceit casing itself safely in a confined sense of high sophistication; the uncertainty as to whether one is serious or not taking itself for ironic pose.'

Leavis had considerable success. A new generation of literary editors looked to him for guidance. By the Sixties the literary columns of the *Guardian* were a Leavisite preserve. To be a man of letters was cause for reproach. The critic must now work in a university. It became fashionable among intellectuals to dismiss Bloomsbury as unworthy of consideration by anyone who was serious or concerned about the plight of our culture.

And then the tide turned. Michael Holroyd had every reason to be proud that his biography of Lytton Strachey turned it. Leavis had ousted biography from criticism: the text alone mattered, the living author was irrelevant, an unwelcome guest, apt to distort the critic's judgement. Holroyd made readers think of Bloomsbury not as a concept but as people. They were no longer cultural symbols. The young of the Sixties and Seventies, so intent on liberating themselves, suddenly found that these old fogies had anticipated them. And when they read of Carrington killing herself from grief, unable to live now that Lytton was dead, they thought Bloomsbury showed an intensity that their critics lacked. The most powerful influence in releasing Bloomsbury from the pillory and replacing them by the lay figures of living human beings was the work of Quentin and Olivier Bell in organizing the Woolf archive from which the biography of Virginia, her diaries and the letters were written and edited.

The four great figures in Bloomsbury have had the luck to find in recent years biographers who are sympathetic without being soupy and who understand what was the point of their lives. Bloomsbury is now as immortal as the circle round August Wilhelm Schlegel in Berlin or that round the Goncourts in Paris or that round Lady Gregory in Dublin. No circle, not Georgiana, Duchess of Devonshire's set, not the Pre-Raphaelites, can match the fascination of the intellectuals and artists who lived and talked in Bloomsbury at the beginning of the century.

1
BLOOMSBURY PAINTERS

VANESSA BELL

Margaret Drabble

VANESSA BELL should need no introduction. She was a painter: she was a daughter, wife, mother, lover; she was Virginia Woolf's sister. She was the pivotal member, almost the matriarch, of the heavily documented Bloomsbury group. In Bloomsbury itself and at Charleston she reigned and painted and provided the centre of an intimate yet extended circle of friends and relatives. And yet her identity has remained more obscure than that of her famous sister. Perhaps she played too many roles. Virginia Woolf was a writer first and foremost; Vanessa Bell was more modest, more self-effacing, less certain about her art, more willing to let it take second place. It is the width of her experience that makes her so attractive a model to women today. Virginia Woolf, in a more traditional, austere, feminist mode, committed herself to her books, at some sacrifice to herself, and, as she herself feared, to those who loved her. Vanessa Bell managed to work, produce children, run a large household, entertain, all without giving any appearance of overwhelming strain. She managed; she organized; she saved for herself, efficiently, a time and a place to work, despite the constant claims on her attention – 'Nessa will do it' was the constant refrain in her household.

She learned to manage early. As she describes in her Memoir, when her mother and half-sister died, she was left to run a large Victorian household for her exacting and moody father, Leslie Stephen. She was seventeen. It is fashionable to belittle the labours of Victorian housewives who, it is well known, had large numbers of servants to clean and carry water and stoke fires and cook. Nevertheless, most women, if they were honest, would admit that they would rather whisk round with the vacuum cleaner and rush down to the grocery store before a day's work than struggle with a household full of possibly not very co-operative cooks, housemaids, parlour maids and tweenies. For Vanessa Stephen the woman's role came early:

she had to do things the way they had always been done, and to account for every penny. When she and her brothers and sister kept their own house in Bloomsbury, the experience of Hyde Park Gate must have been invaluable. She knew prices, how and what to order, how to balance her books. She also learned negative lessons from her father's household: that it was important to be comfortable, to make other people comfortable. The relief of shaking off the dust sheets of the Victorian age, of abandoning the straight-backed chairs and straight-backed poses, the shrouded pianos and plush-framed photographs, breathes through everything the sisters write about their childhood and their escape from it. Vanessa learned to make people feel easy, as she herself on her visits to grand houses and even in her own home had not been able to feel. She learned, in fact, to be the good hostess that, in her father's and her half-brother George Duckworth's terms, she so resolutely refused to be. One has only to see a corner of a room painted by her at Charleston, or a studio scene painted in Gordon Square, to recognize a whole world of informality, physical well-being, light, activity. She was not a tidy person. Her home always looked 'lived-in', but always accommodating, always alive.

She continued to have servants, of course. There are stories suggesting that her servants were slightly more eccentric than those of Hyde Park Gate: the greatest problem was to find a cleaning woman who would not tidy away unfinished still life compositions. But she was quite good at doing things herself: the shelves she put up were not very elegant, but they served. She learned to drive a car, because she had to; her husband, Clive, did not. She gardened, again rather at random: she was one of the first to treat the globe artichoke as a flower rather than as a mere vegetable. Her method of stretching canvases struck her son Quentin as inefficient and laborious, but it served. She strikes one as an amateur of the domestic life, good at improvisation, enjoying the random results of purchases of furniture, curtains, bits and pieces. Her flower arrangements and her garden must have been as she painted them: abundant, casual, colourful, curiously overflowing. It is extraordinary how strikingly distinctive even a corner of a Charleston room appears in a painting. She and Duncan Grant painted Charleston for decades, and the spirit of the house leaves its stamp on a still life of two bottles and a glass, on a jar, on a painted chair.

Virginia Woolf, in *A Room of One's Own*, describes, in a controversial passage, the power and creativity of the domestic impulse in women. She says:

> One goes into the room – but the resources of the English language would be much put to the stretch, and whole flights of words would need to wing their way illegitimately into existence before a woman could say what happens when she goes into a room. The rooms differ so completely; they are calm or thunderous; open on to the sea, or, on the contrary, give on to a prison yard; are hung with washing; or alive with opals and silks; are hard as horsehair or soft as feathers – one has only to go into any room in any street for the whole of that extremely complex force of femininity to fly in one's face. How should it be otherwise? For women have sat indoors all these millions of years, so that by this time the very walls are permeated by their creative force . . .

In Vanessa Bell this creative force worked harmoniously rather than in conflict with the domestic impulse. As her sister in words, she in paint was a great creator of interiors, and of domestic architecture: homes, rooms, houses, gardens seen, often (as in *To the Lighthouse*) through windows. Her impulse to paint was inextricably connected with her feeling about her surroundings: she used to shop in local junk shops for old bits of furniture, beds, chairs, boxes, and then cover them with paintings. She painted fireplace tiles, bed-heads, boxes for records, plates and cups. Works of art, like pots and plates made by Roger Fry, were for daily use, not simply for decoration. She and Duncan Grant decorated with murals rooms for several of their friends, in London, Cambridge, Sussex: photographs still record the invention, the spirit, the sense of ease with which she confronted large-scale tasks so often thought unsuitable for women. There was nothing small and cosy about her domestic creativity: it was large and bold.

Her connection with the Omega Workshops, founded by Roger Fry, is also an expression of this impulse in her: her designs for textiles, tiles, furnishing fabrics, tables, are among some of the most successful of her work. It would be easy and indeed accurate to categorize this part of her work as 'decorative' and 'feminine'. All that one needs is to wipe out the pejorative tone, belligerently to declare, along with Virginia Woolf, that female art may be different but is certainly not necessarily inferior to male. There is a great deal of rage in Virginia's work on this theme, rage which she herself considered destructive, but remarkably little in Vanessa's. On the contrary, there is a confidence, a positive acceptance, at least in the early work: it seems not to have crossed her mind much that her work could be categorized pejoratively as feminine. The positive spirit is too strong: so her art is domestic, she paints domestic objects, but did not Cézanne, Van Gogh, Vuillard, Bonnard do the same?

Virginia's attitude to her own womanhood was, as we know from her novels and diary, far from happy: she believed in an androgynous artistic ideal, in the embodying of both male and female impulses in the one person. There is nothing at all androgynous about Vanessa Bell. She was not only a home-maker: she was also a passionately emotional woman, and a passionate mother. Her first love was Jack Hills, the widower of her half-sister Stella: the love came to nothing, and anyway the two would not have been allowed to marry, as in those days a man was not, curiously, permitted to marry his deceased wife's sister. In 1907 she married Clive Bell, by whom she had two sons: Julian born in 1908 and Quentin in 1910. The marriage was in many ways successful. To the end they remained close, sharing a good deal if not all; and certainly she suffered from none of the sexual complexity and frigidity that made her sister's life so difficult. Both married friends who were also intellectual companions, but whereas Leonard Woolf had to look after Virginia, Vanessa needed no looking after. Physically, she found life straightforward. The Victorian ogre of sex did not terrify her: she was in her element in the free discussions and jokes and frankness that were part of Bloomsbury's distinctive intellectual atmosphere. She betrays none of the reticence so noticeable, and so nobly self-explained, in Virginia's work. A well-balanced, handsome woman, free of conventions and at home in her own body; or so she strikes one.

She was a devoted mother, and adored her children. She never recovered from the shock of the death of her eldest, Julian, and her daughter Angelica believes that it was this that caused her gradual withdrawal from life, her retreat into a small, safe, familiar circle. She had suffered much anxiety also over Quentin as a baby, and, as she relates in her Memoir of Roger Fry, it was Fry's sympathy over her otherwise unshared and unappreciated maternal anxiety that drew them together and into the affair that stimulated her so much as an artist. Her third child, Angelica, was the offspring of her third and greatest love, Duncan Grant, who was to live and work with Vanessa for the rest of her life, sharing a home and friends, painting the same objects. Angelica, considerably younger than her brothers, recalls that her childhood, for one brought up in so unconventional a household, was oddly Victorian. She had a nanny, and was 'brought down' from the nursery to see her mother at tea time. This recollection sums up a curious ambiguity in Vanessa Bell's attitude towards her own liberated life. Even by modern standards her life strikes one as unconventional and courageous. Yet she retained a respect for the conventions. Talk was restrained in front of the children: *risqué* jokes were made in Latin. Angelica was expected to disappear to the nursery when required.

By any standards, Vanessa's life has a pioneering quality: she is a positive model, in an area where there are few, and the spontaneous joy with which she expressed herself is in welcome contrast with the more hard-won victories of others. She was not a martyr to emancipation: if she compromised, it was possibly through a desire to make things more comfortable for others, rather than through fear of public opprobrium.

But, of course, the most important fact about her is that she was a painter. I approach a description of her work with the greatest diffidence, for like most educated English people I have had no visual education at all, and am quite unqualified to analyse or judge her work. I do so not as an expert but as an amateur and enthusiast.

There have been relatively few women painters. There are some distinguished names, some better known to art historians than to the general public: Artemesia Gentileschi, an outstanding and much-commissioned member of the Caravaggisti, Vigée Le Brun, Angelica Kauffmann and, more recently, Berthe Morisot, Marie Laurencin, Mary Cassatt, Margaret and Frances MacDonald, Käthe Kollwitz, Gwen John, Laura Knight. And there have been some important and interesting names in book illustration. But the list lacks the indisputable authority of a list which includes Jane Austen, George Eliot, Emily Dickinson, the

Brontës, Virginia Woolf. It is striking that, whereas most of the writers mentioned led solitary lives, the painters were on the whole wives, daughters, sisters or mistresses of other painters. Painting seems to depend more on practical apprenticeship and physical connection than writing, and in a painting fraternity women seem to have been more able and willing to accept the role of partner and mistress: Georgiana Burne-Jones used to cut her husband's blocks, but one cannot imagine Charlotte Brontë sharpening her husband's pen. Occasionally women have outpaced their male helpmate: Artemesia Gentileschi's paintings were bigger, bolder and bloodier than her father's, most now prefer Gwen John to Augustus John. But Vanessa Bell was modest about her work, content to take second place. One cannot imagine that Virginia Woolf would ever have felt modesty about her own work: although she was sensitive to attack, she was also amazingly confident of her own worth. Indeed, one feels that she is sensitive to attack not because she fears it might be just, but because she knows it to be unjust or ignorant; and is as much enraged as hurt by it. Vanessa, valuing herself less highly, more sensitive perhaps on behalf of those she loved than on her own account, seems to have responded to criticism less aggressively.

This does not imply that she was a half-hearted painter. On the contrary, she was committed to the career from early childhood, as Virginia was to writing. Unlike her husband, she was not a rebel from a family of Philistines, but a member of a family which had always loved the arts and encouraged artistic promise. Her father was a writer, from a family of writers; her mother was painted by the most famous of Victorian painters, George Frederic Watts, who was a great friend of her great-aunt, the famous photographer, Julia Cameron. Between 1901 and 1904 she attended the Royal Academy Schools, where she studied for a time under Sargent. Her earliest surviving work, a portrait, dates from 1905. She exhibited first in 1908. But her finest work is generally considered to be that which she produced after the celebrated Post-Impressionist Exhibition of 1910, and after she began to feel the influence of Roger Fry. During the First World War, undeterred by the breaking of nations (most of her friends were pacifists and disapproved strongly of the war), undistracted by her children and rising above the challenge of providing a Sussex refuge and home for what seems like a remarkably large shifting Bloomsbury population, she managed to paint, with a new boldness and freedom, with invention and confidence, works which now strike one as wholly original.

Her reputation has been dimmed for several reasons: partly because later artists, such as Ben Nicholson, rose to prominence and led movements which attracted great critical attention, partly because some of her later work (for example, her portraits of grandchildren) could legitimately be accused of sentimentality, partly because literary Bloomsbury fell out of fashion in the aggressive Forties and Fifties and artistic Bloomsbury suffered the same fate. But if one looks back to the works painted in the second decade of the century, one can see undiminished the power and creativity of her best work. In the Tate Gallery there is an abstract painting, painted *c.*1914, which demonstrates, as Richard Morphet says, 'the extreme degree of abstraction achieved at this period in the Bloomsbury Circle'. There are interiors, portraits, still lifes which show her experiments with Cubism and Post-Impressionism, and the influence of Fauve painting: Roger Fry and Clive Bell had brought the inspiration of the Continent to insular England, and she was one of the first to profit. The portrait of the actress Iris Tree, painted in 1915, is large, bold, confident, with a startling use of colour: not at all a 'woman's' painting. Her interior, 'The Bedroom, Gordon Square', painted in 1912, is a remarkable composition: subdued, even bleak, yet full of energy.

Trying to describe paintings in words is a thankless task. The works themselves are still to be seen. There have been recent exhibitions in London, new acquisitions in the Tate, and critics and admirers from a new generation have rediscovered her work. Richard Morphet (the fortunate possessor of the Iris Tree portrait) has praised her 'gravity, audacity and joyous fantasy, her bold modernity and passionate response to the past, her vigour and richness, her strong formal intelligence'. André Dunoyer de Segonzac, in a foreword to a 1961 exhibition, says 'Never in her work does one meet with those affected prettinesses, too common in feminine art, nor yet with the facile but seductive picturesque: all is purity, frankness and perfect simplicity both in what is expressed and the means of expression.' There is little to add, except one's personal response: in my case, a response to a life-style breathing through both subject matter and treatment, an admiration for the essentially positive and harmonious nature of her portraits, her still lifes, her decorative art. The life of Charleston, with drinks on the mantelpiece, flowers and thistles in a vase, and Vanessa Bell combining work and her hostess-role by offering to paint the less restless of her guests, offers a peculiarly satisfactory and comforting image. Some critics have reacted strongly against the apparent privilege, the apparent ease, the small private income, the lack of involvement in outside events. But the image is sufficiently powerful, the talents sufficiently great, to outweigh and outlast attack. Few nowadays think of Virginia Woolf, one of the great innovators in the art of the novel, as the mandarin highbrow Bloomsbury queen that Wyndham Lewis cruelly portrayed, and people are beginning to appreciate that Vanessa Bell was much greater than the sensitive feminine conventional painter of conventional subjects that she was considered in the Fifties. Some of her later paintings may well have been sentimental, but one has only to look at her last self-portrait to read another story.

To me she is a painter of inner space. Her rooms, her interiors, her chairs and pots and drooping flowers, her use of one of her favourite colours, that strange dusky pink, add up to an impression of a strong, confident inner life. Virginia Woolf wrote an essay attacking the notion of woman as the angel in the house, but there are many kinds of angels. One would not wish to set Vanessa Bell up as mother figure, but her works certainly describe a motivating, all pervading spirit. Not a wholly untroubled one: there is something rather alarming about the serenity of Duncan Grant's later portraits of her, suggesting a formidable self-contained strength. She looks like the woman she was, a woman well accustomed to life, well learned in organizing herself in both easy and tragic times, a woman who relies on herself, first and foremost, and expects others to rely on her. A woman who succeeded in combining many roles, and whose work and life yet manage to present a harmonious unity. Yeats said that we must choose between perfection of the life or of the work, a sentiment that Virginia Woolf would have well understood. In Vanessa Bell, the two, owing to miracles of discipline and hard work on her part, appear not to have been in conflict.

DUNCAN GRANT AS STAGE DESIGNER

Asya Chorley

DUNCAN GRANT the decorator is visible in every available surface at Charleston: fireplaces, walls, table-tops and doors are disguised with vigorous shapes, contours softened by muted colours. The whole interior is almost a stage set for a play. There is perhaps more to be found in these and other examples of his decorative work than in the often sombre and overworked easel paintings. Paradoxically, the requirements of working in a confined space or in a situation which was already dominated by an existing framework, rather than subduing Grant's imagination, appear to have stimulated it, encouraging him to improvise and develop his use of colour.

Although much, then, is known of Grant's work as a furniture, textile and ceramic designer, comparatively little attention has been paid to his work in the theatre. The problem partly lies with the transitory nature of the theatre itself. There are few examples of his stage designs and these are often undocumented, so only impressions can be deduced from the rare photographs of performances and from contemporary criticism. However, by considering his work for the theatre one gains not only an understanding of the extent of his role as a decorator/designer but also an insight into a controversial period of theatrical history.

Little is known of Grant's first foray into the theatre – a project to design the sets and costumes for Harley Granville-Barker's production of *Macbeth* in 1912 which never materialized. But in the same year, partly as a result of the seminal Second Post-Impressionist Exhibition, Grant was provided with his first real opportunity to design for the stage. In an effort to assist a reluctant English audience in the understanding of French art Roger Fry had invited the director Jacques Copeau from Paris to lecture, during the exhibition, on French literature. Copeau, who was to become one of the outstanding new French directors, found himself in sympathy with the views and aspirations of Fry and his associates. They shared a dislike of pretension and excess while firmly believing in the virtue of simplicity and the importance of the relationship between form and colour. Copeau detected in Grant's work which had been included in the exhibition qualities which he considered would contribute to the new image he was aiming to establish for the French theatre.

Copeau was one of the new revolutionary group of directors who sought to establish homogeneity in the theatre, believing a balance should be achieved between each aspect of a production. The role of scene design was to underline, subtly, the meaning of a play, not to overstate it with clumsy attempts at Realism which had dominated nineteenth-century theatre. Following the trend established by Diaghilev, Copeau realized that the artist rather than the professional scene painter might translate his ideas. In the summer of 1913, when Fry, Grant and Vanessa Bell were embarking on the experiment of the Omega Workshops, Copeau commissioned Grant to design the sets and costumes for his production of *Twelfth Night* to be presented at his recently opened Théâtre du Vieux Colombier. Grant worked with great enthusiasm, producing the designs within ten days, for which he received a fee of £20. The costumes proved to be a direct reflection of his art, and many were made of Omega fabrics. The production had its *première* in May 1914 and was to become one of Copeau's greatest successes, with 187 performances; both director and critics recognized Grant's contribution. The collaboration continued and in 1917 Copeau commissioned designs from Grant for a production of *Pelléas et Mélisande* presented in New York in 1918. Vanessa Bell helped him with the making up of the costumes, an aspect of the theatre in which, like many artists, he was totally uninterested. That was not his only difficulty as an artist working in the theatre. In 1921 Grant started work on designs for a production of Gide's play *Saul*. But Copeau was unable to tolerate his absence from Paris and the theatre, and Grant was reluctant to be at the beck and call of the director so the professional collaboration came to an end.

Grant's experience with Copeau and the Omega Workshops confirmed his opinion that the modern movement was not confined to painting. In his productions since 1910 Diaghilev had been largely responsible for enabling contemporary artists, notably Picasso, to reach a wider audience with designs for his ballets. In 1919 the Russian Ballet returned to London with two important additions to their repertory – *La Boutique Fantasque* (with designs by André Derain) and *Le Tricorne*, Picasso's second work for Diaghilev. Artists, performers and their mentor were enthusiastically welcomed by Bloomsbury. This connection was later to be strengthened by Lydia Lopokova's marriage to Maynard Keynes. Knowing Diaghilev's keenness to exploit the new, Grant had high hopes that an 'Omega' ballet would be commissioned, for which he would provide the costumes and Roger Fry the sets. Although this never materialized, it may have been some consolation when Leonide Massine, Diaghilev's former leading dancer, invited Grant to design *Togo; or the Noble Savage*, which was presented in the Stoll review *You'd be Surprised* at Covent Garden in January 1923. The participants had all been connected with the Russian Ballet; the main roles were performed by Massine and Lopokova, to music by Milhaud. But this artistic pedigree did not guarantee critical success. *The Curtain* complained of the waste of the dancers in 'a ballet which was no bally good' and *The Times* was equally condemning: 'On the principle of "least said, soonest mended", silence is probably the most fitting commentary . . .' However, *Dancing Times* did at least recognize Grant's contribution, praising 'a truly Mexican opulence of colour in the costumes, Woizikowsky being radiant in orange and different characters . . . providing a sufficient capacity for colour'. Grant's second and last collaboration with Massine and Lopokova was on a short *pas de deux* 'The Postman', produced at the Coliseum in April 1925, for which he provided the costumes and backcloth. This simple *divertissement* proved popular and Grant's design for the backcloth, with its patterned border of fruit reminiscent of Omega decoration, was considered worthy of being included in *The Studio*'s survey 'Design in the Theatre' (published in 1927, plate 59).

It was perhaps inevitable that when Lytton Strachey finally agreed to the special charity performance of his play *The Son of Heaven* at the Scala Theatre in July 1925 he should ask his friend Duncan to design the costumes and sets. This 'Chinese concoction' was considered 'a moderate success'. Although it was generally agreed that the best features were the sets and the music by Walton, there was some confusion among the critics as to whether Grant drew his inspiration from Picasso's *Parade* or the D'Oyly Carte *Mikado*.

Duncan Grant's most notable work for the theatre was a result of his association with the Camargo Society. The Society came into existence after the death of Diaghilev in 1929. Its aim was not to create a substitute for the Russian Ballet but to promote talented British dancers and designers. The Committee was led by Lopokova and Arnold Haskell. The Society represented the first serious British attempt to produce ballet in London's West End. Its most prestigious season took place at the Savoy Theatre in June 1932. Grant's involvement was due to his friendship with the choreographer Rupert Doone, whose ballet *The Enchanted Grove*, with designs by Grant, was included in the 1932 season. It was one of the impressive array of new ballets which included *Façade*, *Rio Grande* (designs by Burra) and *High Yellow* (designs by Vanessa Bell).

It is interesting that *The Enchanted Grove* was yet another production with an exotic theme. Clearly Grant's style was considered an important contribution in the attempt to create an alien magical atmosphere. The reviews were mixed. One critic dismissed it as 'a ghastly piece of Rococo Chinoiserie', but others commended Grant '. . . Duncan Grant's scenery and dresses for this ballet are most successful' and 'Above all, Duncan Grant's costumes and *décor* for the Ravel ballet had distinction and grip.'

It is likely that the majority of the audience shared one critic's prejudice that 'The classics more than hold their own against the newcomers', for the most popular ballets in the season were *Giselle* and *Swan Lake*. Surprisingly Grant provided the scenery for the latter, but his touch of originality was recognized '. . . the new *décor* by Duncan Grant substitutes sepia graces for the old familiar mere with its coroneted swimmers'. Despite the mixed responses, the 1932 Savoy season was of great significance, for it firmly established British ballet and provided British artists with a rare opportunity to design for the stage.

After the Camargo Society productions Grant did no work for the theatre for over two decades. It is possible that this was a result of his preoccupation with interior decoration and industrial design during the Thirties and Forties. But it is also likely that there was little opportunity; the Camargo Society proved exceptional in encouraging artists to design for the stage. George Sheringham, in an article in *The Studio*, attacked the indifference of the majority of theatre managers:

> How pleasant to have written of how the designers are gaining greater and wider experience of the many problems they are asked to solve, or again, of how the theatre is keeping pace in its decoration with the modern movement . . . But the distressing fact is that I found the designers in their studios – decoration in the English theatre is still, for the greater part, bound in a tradition, not old but bad . . .

Sheringham goes on to mention Grant's and others' 'good work at some of the London theatres; when on the rare occasions it has been decided to employ an artist for a change'.

Grant did not return to the theatre until 1956, when he designed sets and costumes for John Blow's opera/masque *Venus and Adonis*, presented at the Aldeburgh Festival that year. And this commission only came about as a result of his friendship with Britten and Pears.

It is sad that British theatre managers did not show the same courage and imagination as other commercial enterprises such as Shell, Cunard and Foley China, who were prepared to give Grant and other contemporary artists the opportunity to experiment with design. Although Grant's stage designs may have suffered from his tendency to be over-exuberant, his love of movement, as is shown in the frequent appearance of dancers and acrobats in his painting and decorative work, and his very personal use of colour, were qualities which could have contributed to the reputation of British stage design if circumstances had allowed.

REMEMBERING DUNCAN AND VANESSA

Lawrence Gowing

I FIND THAT I have engaged to discuss something rather personal. But it was very much to the point for me when I sat down on a wet Bank holiday to think about remembering Duncan and Vanessa, and in doing so immediately discovered how very far the roots of thought extended into the compost of my life. It was to the point; or at least towards the point, that the branching rootlets rambled and groped, because in the achievement of no more far-reaching exploration than this they already discovered that not my thought only but, I verily believe, the reflections of almost anyone born in the second decade, the teens, of the century, who had made his or her way toward the visual arts, were likely to concern the same part of London and the same very small group of people.

I acquit myself hurriedly, or at least hopefully, of the accusation that this observation is in itself parochial, if only because this is in the common view, which I hold to still, no accusation at all. It is a fact of cultural ecology that the favourable climate in which to grow towards the fine arts was for a period of more than a century that which prevailed in rather few streets running on either side of an axis north and south between two famously beautiful, though barely even respectable (certainly far from genteel), London squares, and lying in general west of the east sides of three or four others more securely domestic, the conditions – that is to say – in a strip of the town of which the extent would be vastly exaggerated by identifying it even with half of a square mile to the east of St Marylebone and west of St Pancras and sadly, though not fatally, misnamed by calling it after the Russell estates in Bloomsbury; misnamed because the conditions in the area, which I think has only in retrospect been known at all widely as Fitzrovia, were precisely those that attracted the artists, and among them those who concern us particularly today, who were in the nature of refugees from one or other habitat to the west and the east, which was socially and morally more accountable, though in any visual culture null and void.

If an idea or even an experience of conditions in Fitzrovia that were uniquely beneficial and favourable to the fine arts seems now to be merely imaginary, I would parenthetically direct you to the literature of this townscape, which I hold blessed, a great part of it anecdotal – I have in mind *The Life and Times of Joseph Nollekens*, with the anecdotal appendix, the same author's *Book for a Rainy Day*, as well as the unashamedly self-indulgent *Wine and Walnuts*. Three at least of the books written by that one-man archive of British art, J.T. Smith, the first Keeper of Prints and Drawings at the Britain Museum, have in some of these streets enriched nearly every house with the record of the life and art that flourished there.

I meditate on history, not entirely from habit, but because in order to cast any light of my own on our present subjects I have first to explain how natural it was that the eighteen-year-old son of a Hackney draper should have come, without serious hope of professional qualification – or even any thought that such a thing existed – to study painting in the studio opened at 12 Fitzroy Street by four premature post-Modernists, whose steps he dogged morning, noon and night, out of loyal, indeed dog-like, devotion, up and down the self-same street, which became for him – the present speaker – a street in paradise: such is adolescence. It was in a dusty midday in that very autumn of 1937 that my three admired friends, on the way from a morning's painting at 12 Fitzroy Street, paused on seeing the two figures at the door of No.8, as if to salute two people known to me until then only by repute. One was a man of classic yet elfin beauty, from whom there issued an unassuming yet perceptive sympathy that was its precious essence. With him there was a woman so stately that she would have inspired awe, if a friendliness in her Gothic beauty had not been so unfailingly generous and gracious. Such were Duncan Grant and Vanessa Bell, as I first and superficially observed them. My friends were deferential but very ready for lunch and soon on their way to a table up the street. One of them, a painter-critic originally from South Africa, who was by then a refugee from New Cavendish Street, identified Duncan to me: 'At your age I would have given an arm to have seen Duncan Grant as you have just seen him. That will give you an idea of how fortunate you are.'

It did indeed give me an idea, even though I was still at an age that had no respect for anyone, except for the first painters to whom I had attached myself, and for whom I feel the same admiration to this day. If Fitzroy Street seemed to be paved with the pure gold of commitment to painting, it was Vanessa and Duncan who had in effect laid what turned out to be magic paving for the boy from Oakleigh Park. I should like to recapture the atmosphere of life in that street and what it owed to the couple in No.8: to know it and know them was for me a transporting experience. In Fitzroy Street, before the old houses were destroyed, you could feel an apostolic continuity in the perspective that led from the Percy Street corner, where the Eiffel Tower had catered for a genuine British *avant-garde*, to the Euston Road half a mile away. Constable's house, with its little gallery leading into the studio, was at 75 Charlotte Street; the studio at 8 Fitzroy Street had served Sickert, and Whistler before him. Round the corner, facing the Yorkshire Grey, the neat little studio house in which my friends and I rented a room in turn, was the very house to which Thomas Jones had returned from Naples in 1783. The broad street had a skyline of uniquely Continental character, punctuated by the spire of the Swiss church. The then uncluttered breadth of the street from kerb to kerb, the precipitous height of the sharp-etched eaves, and the radiance that the leaking roof-lights scooped out of the sky; such impressions were all different in those days, and I have not known the like of them again. But then, one does not pass through an enchanted adolescence twice. I was half aware, even then, that the witching spell was worked from No.8.

Through the ever-open front door and the echoing hallway, one mounted half a flight of stone stairs and faced a glass door giving apparently on to the canyon of empty, windy space at the back of the house. At one's ring, a distant step was already tapping along the clattering passage that crossed the void, to open a welcome not more than very slightly distraught by the interruption – it is a mercy that adolescents are forgiven their tactlessness. One was led without complaint, even with a pensive welcome, back along the iron corridor, bowing now and swaying somewhat, on the way to one or other of the great grey studios, past the aromatic kitchens along the back. In retrospect, there seems always to have been a near-masterpiece on the easel. Memorably and invariably there was a model on the couch, arrayed with an exotic gaudiness to scandalize the self-righteous austerity to which I held. Often it was Angelica herself, my contemporary and fellow student, as well as my friend for ever, who contrived to lodge my family and me across the field from Charleston only a few years ago, Angelica who then, with her mocking severity, contrived to teach me the continuing lesson, that the awe which my brashness did not hide was no more than expected, if not exacted, from a creature no less juvenile but much less polished than she was herself. The generosity with which I was then received, the apparent seriousness with which opinions that I did not know I possessed were debated, gave me a confidence above my station, which I have not lost.

When I was presented to Vanessa and Duncan, perhaps on that very autumn day in 1937, when we gathered as if before an apostolic podium outside No.8 on the way to lunch, they were perhaps already thinking of how to raise funds for the School of Drawing and Painting, which my friends had opened down the street. Vanessa watched over the school with a quite motherly attention. We read in Mrs Spalding's controversial but useful book that she wrote to Quentin: 'They have about 15 students and everyone is happy and cheerful.' The school, where I remember at least Vanessa teaching devotedly, meant a good deal to her; at that moment it helped to fill a hole in her life, and her ways of helping, which were countless and unstinted, included the grandest party that I had ever attended, held in the Fitzroy Street studios at that Christmas, a function that meant everything to me, since it was the occasion on which I began to my surprise to sell my pictures – in the first instance to a patron of such noted discernment that it was never again thought that I might become an insurance clerk, which was to have been my destination in the new year.

I knew Duncan before the War, and after it Vanessa, rather slightly, you may claim hardly well enough to dilate upon my memories of either. Yet I do remember one thing about them which seems to have escaped some people who were acquainted with them over a much longer span of years. So far as I and my friends were concerned, their record was one of extraordinary generosity and of a peculiarly selfless enlightenment. They supported and promoted – and enjoyed – styles of painting between Coldstream and Pasmore and a train of very purposeful thought about painting, which might seem to have been at opposite extremes to their own. On consideration, after dwelling for a day or two on my memories of them, I am convinced that any such idea would misinterpret both contributions to this peculiarly productive *entente*. In the last years of Roger Fry's life – he died three years before that noted party – he was giving an altogether different value to the sensations of nature from that which they possessed in his aesthetic before. In his last book he remarked that Turner seemed never to have had an original pictorial sensation of his own. You may not like that view – Pasmore would not, though I remember Graham Bell writing something rather like it. The fact remains that these years were characterized, and not only in England, by a growing distrust of subjectivity which marked for a time a wide variety of styles and theories, leaving the romantic and surrealist trains of thought increasingly isolated. Helen Anrep used to say that Roger Fry would have welcomed Coldstream's innovation in this light, and always lamented that they did not come together. She was in the best position to venture such a guess. I used to discuss with Duncan the very low position given to innovation in my own juvenile view of art. When he made his way up to the top floor of No.6, where I by then had one of the back studios, looking down on the two slate pyramids at No.8, I remember, tactless as ever, throwing open my door and engaging him with conversation and coffee. I was conceited enough to feel strengthened in my view by his comment that he welcomed the shift of opinion away from the requirement to innovate for innovation's sake. It may seem that the young painter and the elder were both talking considerable nonsense for social reasons, but it is worth noticing that at that moment opinion was forming round Duncan and Vanessa similar to the opinion round Derain in France. There was passion, antagonism, even enmity, there was that icy concern for linear integrity which Ingres called the probity of art. Before the end there were ironies and to spare. The fiercest enemy from Omega days ended by warning his readers against the Demon of Progress in the Arts, perhaps the single piece of recent criticism with which Duncan and Vanessa could have wholeheartedly agreed.

When the visitors were ebbing like a tide (as exhibition visitors do) at closing time from Duncan's great exhibition at the Tate, I was suddenly aware that his art was truly, *musically* polychromatic, in a respect that I had never properly understood. Coming up beside Duncan, both of us reluctant to lose the last minute, I burst out: 'There is so much in it of Delacroix!' With that sweet straightforwardness, yet faltering somewhat, and twittering with gratification, he answered 'Why are you surprised? I like Delacroix!' Going out into the evening I knew that we must revalue the sense of apostolic succession all over again.

The houses have gone: the straight streets, Charlotte and Fitzroy, will never be themselves again and the plaque to Verlaine and Rimbaud in Howland Street was never replaced in the Post Office tower. But Charleston we have, open to be enjoyed as it could never have been in their day, because, I can't forbear to point out, it was then far from accessible, but rather a forbidden shrine to the necessary exclusiveness of the artists' life. Vanessa herself was held to be, how sensibly, forbidding, and Duncan's enchanting accessibility and straightforwardness were equipped with a special elusiveness.

The important thing – and I do not know anywhere better to feel this than at Charleston – is that the studio consensus is never nonsense. In a place like Charleston you can really see the sinews that hold the past to the future. That house is not only a beautiful thing, a profoundly desirable public possession for ever, which we positively must hand on, strengthened, enriched and materially secure for our children. It is beautiful in its expression of a profound truth that cannot be expressed in any other way. The substance of tradition is social, real human sociability. One cannot imagine Vanessa or Duncan supporting one kind of painting at the expense of another. When Vanessa spoke in her grave deep voice, in whose timbre the immanence of love and laughter always lurked, one was in no doubt that it was the beauty of painting that she held dear, as we must hold and keep it now. It is a domestic beauty, like a family feeling: that is why it is felt to much advantage in that house. At Charleston we are always in Vanessa's presence – with attention we can imagine the amorous spell, which alone held together such an improbable community for so long. Vanessa and Duncan identified it so completely with a visible harmony that everyone carried and carries away something different, something more intimate than any other art or place.

THE OMEGA WORKSHOPS

Judith Collins

THE ART critic of the *Observer*, P.G. Konody, writing his weekly column in December 1913, had occasion to draw his readers' attention to an unusual sight at one corner of Fitzroy Square, a stately Adam-designed square in the north of Bloomsbury. He wrote of a stir of people gathered outside 33 Fitzroy Square 'arrested by the stains of a diluted Post-Impressionism that has filtered through the wall into vacant spaces on the second floor. These flirting decorations – gay, giddy and slight – might hold their place on some sun-baked wall within the equatorial belt, but . . . they affront the grave decorum of Fitzroy Square.' The 'gay, giddy' decorations to which Konody referred were part of Roger Fry's attempt to court the British public with a new style in art and decoration, a Post-Impressionist style. In the spring of 1913 he took the lease of 33 Fitzroy Square as the headquarters of his Omega Workshops in order to introduce Post-Impressionism into domestic decorations.

Fry had thought up the term Post-Impressionist in the autumn of 1910 when a journalist asked him for a blanket name to cover the recent French art he was about to show to the British public at the Grafton Galleries, London. Fry organized a second Post-Impressionist Exhibition at the same venue in the winter of 1912, and this time he showed recent British art alongside examples of recent French art; thus Duncan Grant and Vanessa Bell's paintings hung in the same show as those of Cézanne, Gauguin, Van Gogh, Matisse, Derain and Picasso. Post-Impressionist art could be characterized by an insistence upon the formal values which make up a painting, stressing those far above the content. What that meant was that for Fry a painting by Cézanne, for example, consisted of a carefully and deeply considered arrangement of shapes, colours, tone and lines, which was more important than the recognition that it portrayed a certain mountain landscape in Provence.

This concern with geometrical shapes and with balances of colour harmony could be taken up and used fruitfully in a decorative context, and a painted table-top or a pair of curtains could show an echo of lessons learnt from Cézanne.

The Omega Workshops was the place where such things could happen. Fry founded the workshops for two main reasons: first, because he wanted to make the British public recognize the importance of Post-Impressionism and the improvement it could bring to the poor level of design and decoration in objects of daily use; and secondly because it could offer a small measure of patronage to the young British artists who had gathered around Fry as a result of his two Post-Impressionist Exhibitions.

The premises at 33 Fitzroy Square acted as showrooms, storerooms for the stock and design studio. Two showrooms with changing stock and murals of 'blue lagoons' painted by Grant and Bell were on the ground floor, along with a small office for the business manager. (There were two business managers during the seven years of the Omega's existence, and Mr Miles, the first manager, even christened his son Omega.) The design studio, on the first floor, benefited from a huge window which allowed in plenty of light, on either side of which on the exterior façade were the gay, giddy painted canvases of Post-Impressionist couples dancing. In the studio artists were provided with paints and paper, and were free to design anything they wished. Fry thought the creative process worked better if left unchecked. Once an artist had executed a design, he placed it unsigned in a portfolio in the studio, and there it remained until Fry or a client, sifting through, found something suitable for a particular purpose. Often a single design could be used for a variety of ends: Duncan Grant produced a design of a vase of flowers and this found its way on to two embroidered firescreens, and a flowing hand-painted silk evening cloak.

Artists were paid thirty shillings a week for three half-days – a good wage for 1913; attendance beyond that was not encouraged, since Fry wanted his artist employees to remain first and foremost painters rather than designers of applied art objects. The Omega decorated and designed a very wide range of domestic objects, murals, mosaic floors, stained-glass windows, tables and chairs, printed and woven linens, dresses, hand-knotted rugs, pottery, toys and small miscellaneous items such as painted glove and pencil boxes, marquetry trays, artificial flowers and outrageously decorated hats. Anything, in fact, that could introduce colour and fresh design into an Edwardian home, which would have been decorated with a narrow range of dark paints and upholstery. Fry felt that a crusade was necessary to bring 'a spirit of fun' into the British interior, and the Omega provided just that.

The Workshops closed in the summer of 1919 for various reasons, notably the expiry of the lease of 33 Fitzroy Square, a shortage of cash and a shortage of young artists. Grant and Bell had moved away from London and the Omega in the spring of 1916; because Grant was a conscientious objector he had to work on the land. In October 1916 they moved into Charleston, which continued to be their home until their respective deaths; the decorative lessons which they had learnt at the Omega they then practised with great panache and fluency upon the walls and furniture there.

Now [in 1984], just over seventy years after the founding of the Omega Workshops, there are to be two major exhibitions of Omega products and related paintings, and these will give us all a marvellous unrepeatable chance to reappraise the contributions of the Workshops to British art and design.

ROGER FRY AND HIS AESTHETIC

Sylvia Stevenson

KENNETH CLARK said of Fry 'in so far as taste can be said to have been changed by one man, it was changed by Roger Fry.' Fry's aesthetic – that part of his over-filled life for which he is today most famous – was his effort to share with others the enormous pleasure he got from looking at paintings and to pass on his vision and understanding. Fundamental to his aesthetic is that he was a deeply committed professional artist, to whom painting was the most important thing in life. He has not been highly regarded as a painter, although there has always been acknowledgement of his skill as a portraitist; but recently there has been a strong increase of interest in other work. As well as a painter he was an art historian, an active and, often, founder member of every major artistic association of his time. He helped launch and direct *The Burlington Magazine*, he mounted the two famous Post-Impressionist Exhibitions of 1910 and 1912, and a great many other exhibitions. He tried his hand at translation (Mallarmé!), he was a tireless talker and lecturer, he was a director for a time of the Metropolitan Museum, he advised on many other collections including the Johnson Collection, now in the Philadelphia Museum. He founded, financed and ran the Omega Workshops from 1913 till their bankruptcy in 1919 – a war casualty.

Fry possessed a number of characteristics that made him into a great critic: he was always eager, everything was 'exciting' (a frequently used Fry word), his absolute integrity was coupled with extreme flexibility and he questioned everyone's opinions, certainly his own. Quentin Bell quoted what Fry said to him once going round a gallery: 'in art we know nothing for certain – consider the Victorians and Landseer. Were they mad or are we blind?' He frequently changed his own mind and never minded saying so. His aesthetic was always in motion:

> I have never believed that I knew what was the ultimate nature of art. My aesthetic has always been a purely practical one, a tentative expedient, an attempt to reduce to some kind of order my aesthetic impressions to date. It has been held merely until such time as fresh experiences might confirm or modify it. Moreover, I've always looked on my system with a certain suspicion. I have recognised that if it ever formed too solid a crust it might stop the inlets of fresh experience . . . so that even in its latest form I do not put forward my system as more than a provisional induction from my own aesthetic experiences.

Added to this flexibility were two other characteristics remarked on by everyone who knew him, an extreme, almost unbelievable, physical energy and his enormous sense of fun. So integrity, supreme energy, sense of fun, flexibility, great inventiveness and, one of the rarest of all gifts, a wonderful detachment from everything but the matter in hand.

Fry until very recently has been associated exclusively with significant form. But to understand Fry's real importance, to understand his influence and to be able to relate it to the 1980s, it is necessary to look further. Indeed there is a very great deal of unpublished material which has still to be digested.

Fry's art criticism falls broadly into three phases, though all are interconnected. His early phase, when he became an acknowledged expert on old masters, particularly Italian. The second, by far the most famous and most discussed and the longest, when he stressed significant form. Lastly, in the final years of his life, the least known, when he walked away from abstraction, back towards his earlier views, when he united and developed both these earlier phases into an exceedingly rich and relevant understanding of what he called 'the double nature of painting'.

Very briefly on Fry's first humanistic phase: he travelled enormously all over Europe but particularly Italy, often on a bicycle, painting and studying. The influence of the Italian masters was very important in shaping his attitudes. The visual simplifications in Fry's early sketch books are very instructive about his still unformulated belief in pure form, even at that early stage.

By 1901 Fry had become a widely respected expert on early

Italian paintings, producing a monograph on Giovanni Bellini and essays on Giotto that are still important today. In 1905 he was in America raising funds for the Burlington and there he had long discussions with Denman Ross, then preparing his book on abstraction. It was about this time that Fry came to his sudden, if late by European standards, but overwhelming appreciation of Cézanne. In 1909 his essay on aesthetics in the *New Quarterly* became the second chapter of *Vision and Design*, published in 1920. The central thesis in *Vision and Design* is that vision is subordinate to design and that the all-important element is form. *Vision and Design* was exceedingly important in Britain, alerting artists to non-European art, already familiar on the Continent, but unknown in Britain until Fry. He discussed the art of the Bushman, negro sculpture, ancient American art, Mohammedan art, Chinese and Islamic art. In his article for the *Athenaeum* of 1920, also republished in *Vision and Design*, on negro sculpture, he wrote:

> We have the habit of thinking that the power to create expressive plastic form is one of the greatest of human achievements, and the names of great sculptors are handed down from generation to generation, so that it seems unfair to be forced to admit that certain nameless savages have possessed this power, not only in a higher degree than we at this moment, but that we as a nation have never possessed it. And yet that is where I find myself.

Henry Moore wrote that reading *Vision and Design* as a student revolutionized his life. 'Once one had read Roger Fry everything was there.' And Moore often spoke of the importance of Cézanne and form in his art.

Fry's statements on pure form are at times exaggerated. He wrote: 'Its all the same to me if I represent Christ or a saucepan, since its the form not the object itself which interests me.' He stated at another point that Rembrandt expressed his profoundest feelings just as well whether he painted the Crucifixion or his mistress. This is Fry's most severe formalist statement, but a year or two later he had modified his position and it was precisely Rembrandt who forced Fry to reconsider his theoretical standpoint. But all his statements on significant form, even the exaggerated ones, must be understood and read in the context of his remark 'I have never believed that

I knew . . .' In any event, formalism was a natural progression, from Wölfflin's *Classic Art* and *Principles of Art History* (greatly admired by Fry), to Bernard Berenson and his tactile values, to Fry and Clive Bell and their significant form.

The third phase of Roger Fry's aesthetic is still little known. Until very recently there has been little reference to it. Benedict Nicolson noted in 1951, at the end of an excellent article on Fry and the Post-Impressionists:

> . . . later Fry turned away from abstraction, seeing in it a denial of artistic sensibility. He could never have pursued significant form to its logical end but was always being lured by inquisitiveness, by that glorious refusal ever to make up his mind which kept him flexible in old age, a stray into rich provinces of the past where pure form was of secondary or even minor importance.

And Quentin Bell, in his Leeds inaugural lecture, said, 'And then from about 1925 he was pulling his own central theory to pieces.' But Fry gave a lecture as a favour to Lytton Strachey's sister, the Mistress of Newnham, in 1931, which has been described to me by a friend who attended it. The lecture was advertised: 'The Henry Sidgwick Memorial Lecture will be given by Mr Roger Fry on November 21st at 5 o'clock in the College Hall. Subject: The Literary Element in Painting.' Roger Fry put on one side of the screen a Dutch interior, Vermeer's 'Milkmaid', and on the other a photograph of a postcard that the Royal Academy had made of this painting in which they had cut a bit off each side. Nothing of importance, so my friend said, had left the picture, but everyone in the audience saw that the form of the painting had been destroyed. Fry went on to explain that he now realized, in his anxiety to get people to look at pictures as works of art and not just illustrations of stories, that he had gone too far in suggesting that form was all that mattered; he intended to atone by writing a book on Rembrandt as a dramatist. Unfortunately he did not live to do so, but he did give two lectures on Rembrandt, which demonstrated that his aesthetic was undergoing very rapid change. The point he had reached just before he died comes across very strongly in another little-known lecture which he gave in Brussels, in French, in 1933 called 'The Double Nature of Painting'. This was not translated and published in this country until March 1969. Fry began by pointing out that music and architecture could be abstract in a way that poetry and painting could not; he discussed the limitations of two-dimensional surfaces, saying that one could not construct either volume or space on a canvas without having recourse to representation. Then an amazing remark from the great proponent of pure form, 'I revert to my idea that in spite of attempts at abstraction, painting has always been, and probably will remain for the great part, a representational art.' Fry pointed out that art criticism had always been the work of men of letters and that this naturally made the literary point of view prevail. He discussed Cicero, he discussed Horace's *Ut pictura poesis* and he said 'this phrase has become a catchword which even 2000 years ago lacked originality'. And a little later he said:

> . . . you have one theory, the literary theory with respect for antiquity, the other, architectural theory, is of quite recent formulation and already I'm starting to modify it. So let us at least ask the question whether there are not two categories of painting. One can be called pure painting, appealing to our emotions, through plastic harmonies as in architecture, and dramatic harmonies as in music, and the other category would contain pictures which make their appeal by the associated ideas and emotions called up by the representation of the objects in a manner corresponding to literature.

Fry then took an extreme example of each. He illustrated a cubist Picasso and said this was more or less pure painting, geometrical forms arranged in a very complicated manner. In contrast he showed Poynter's 'Faithful unto Death' devoid, as far as he could see, of any architectural value. It had no balance in the composition, no significant relationships between the volumes and the spaces, no harmonies between the forms. And then he came to the most difficult part, the consideration of works of art in which we find elements that both appeal to us by plastic harmony on the one hand and move us by association of ideas on the other. He discussed several paintings; interestingly, a Correggio, 'The Martyrdom of St Flavia and St Placid', in which these two elements, he said, pulled in opposite directions.

It is a scene of extreme violence and brutality, expressed

> in forms that compose a harmony, which is not only melodious but voluptuous. It is as if one was to play *Othello* to the music of *Così fan tutte*. For my part I take it as proof of the whole double nature of pictorial art when we find both elements, literary and plastic, as clearly opposed to each other as they are in this instance.

Finally Fry looked at two Masters, who combined both elements harmoniously, Giorgione and Rembrandt. 'It was when looking at 'The Three Philosophers' in Vienna for the first time that I became aware of how much it is necessary to invoke the double function in art in order to explain all that I experience.' And the second painter is Rembrandt, who 'shows such a deep understanding of human nature that if he had not been a painter he would have been one of the great dramatic poets of the world'. He spoke of Rembrandt finding form for himself in the second half of his life. 'His forms, for instance, are far more evocative and less descriptive; masses are more evident, contours are rendered by merely general indications . . .' So he saw both Giorgione and Rembrandt as dually great masters of plastic harmonies and great romantic poets.

Quentin Bell pointed out a truism about Fry. Fry was not perhaps a great painter or even a supremely great writer. His true genius, and it was a genius of the highest order, was revealed when he began to talk. Hundreds of people have spoken as to what Fry meant to them in helping them to art appreciation, but it would be difficult to find a more significant statement than that in the obituary on Roger Fry by E.M. Forster. There is a lesson in it for all of us today.

> If you said to him, 'This must be right, all the experts say so, all the Trustees of the National Gallery say so, all the art-dealers say so, Hitler says so, Marx says so, Christ says so, *The Times* says so', he would in effect reply 'Well, I wonder. Let's see . . .', and you would come away realising that an opinion may be influentially backed and yet be tripe.

A LOOK AT ROGER FRY

Asa Briggs

WHEN I was a sixth former at a northern grammar school I was given a copy of one of the very early Pelican books, the twentieth to appear, Roger Fry's *Vision and Design*. Fry's essays, written over a period of twenty years, came as a revelation to me. My education, good though it was, almost left out visual education altogether. (Fry, I read years later, made the same complaint about his.) It was Fry more than anyone else who made me first think about what we see and what we look at. He drew a distinction between the two. In his very first lines he distinguished sharply also between treating 'ancient works of art' as 'crystallised history' and as 'objects of aesthetic enjoyment'. Was I not already at the age of sixteen guilty of the first inadequacy? Was not everybody I knew in the industrial north of England equally guilty? Bloomsbury was as far away as Tahiti, Giotto as the Bushmen, but I had already read Strachey's *Eminent Victorians* and I knew that Fry's aesthetics were in some way related to Strachey's history. I warmed to much in Fry's book, not least his assertion that his study of the Old Masters for much of his early life was 'never much tainted by archaeological curiosity': 'I tried to study them', he went on, 'in the same spirit as I might study contemporary artists.'

The more I have been drawn myself into a deeper study of history – with visual history put in – the more I have felt the wisdom of those words. The more too, however, I have felt it necessary to learn as much as possible, often through pictures and objects themselves, about the specific historical context in which they were produced. They *are* emissaries. The term 'crystallised history' seems to me wrong: it gets history and its changing interpretations badly wrong.

It is a chastening thought, thinking of history, that there has been a longer time interval between 1938, the year I first heard of Fry, and 1986 than there had been between the date of the first essay in Fry's *Vision and Design*, written in 1917, and the date of publication of John Ruskin's *Fors Clavigera* in 1871. I had read no Ruskin in 1938, but I had seen his house at Coniston. In the *Dictionary of National Biography* Kenneth Clark was to compare Fry with Ruskin. After 1918, he claimed, Fry's position as a critic was established and he became 'incomparably the greatest influence on taste since Ruskin'. To explain the difference between the kinds of influence they exerted – as well as the content of what they had to say (in both cases there were inconsistencies) – it is necessary to examine the specific context. The role of communicators in the nineteenth and twentieth centuries has been quite different. I have never seen any sensitive analysis of this difference in relation to Ruskin and Fry. Art itself, of course, is communication. Both Ruskin and Fry insisted on the point in their lectures, and Fry, drawn early to Ruskin, praised him late in life for his 'prophetic foresight'.

I have recently been thinking more about Ruskin and Fry in seeking to complete a book on *Victorian Things* which I have been writing intermittently for twenty years. It will be the third volume in a trilogy that began with *Victorian People* – I tried *inter alia* in that book to show how misleading Lytton Strachey can be even, perhaps most, when he is most stimulating – and *Victorian Cities*, where I looked at what it is now fashionable to call 'the environment'. Ruskin had much to say about this, much of it memorable, some of the most memorable material in a lecture given at Bradford, near where I was born and recently the subject of an admirable monograph by Dr Hardman. Fry had less to say, although he had one very pertinent aside that 'Pompeii, by-the-by, was a thoroughly Victorian city', and what he had to say was on the whole less interesting than what Morris said or Lethaby. I have been particularly interested, however, in an essay in *Vision and Design*, originally published in 1919, called 'The Ottoman and the Whatnot' which is directly concerned with Victorian things.

Surprisingly enough, Fry already discerned the beginnings of a 'Victorian revival' long before Betjeman or Humphrey House or G.M. Young, pointing to people who were 'hard at work collecting Victorian paper-weights, stuffed humming-birds and wax flowers'. He wrote:

> It is evident, then, that we have just arrived at the point where our ignorance of life in the Victorian period is such as to allow the incurable optimism of memory to build a quite peculiar little earthly paradise out of the boredoms, the snobberies, the cruel repressions, the mean calculations and rapacious speculations of the mid-nineteenth century.

We have long passed the point where historians of Victorian England have ceased to be content with such a massive and comprehensive indictment; and the fact that we have passed it is not because we are more ignorant than we were but because we are more knowledgeable. With all that has been done to explore the ways of life of groups other than the 'upper bourgeoisie', which Fry identified with '*the* Victorian life', we are no longer content with 'a vague and generalised *Stimmung*'. Nor, despite ample popular nostalgia, have we turned it into 'a peculiar little earthly paradise'. The 'process of selection and elimination' has already led to shifts of interest, mood and perception. When I turn back to Victorian things, therefore, I have to put Fry and Ruskin in place as well as the ottoman and the whatnot.

On two points Fry was characteristically sensitive. First, he noted not without appreciation the role of Victorian 'amateurs'. He exaggerated the 'death' of craftsmanship, but he was right to notice the importance of 'invention and experiment': 'we always feel behind everything the capricious fancy of the amateur with his desire to contribute by some joke or conjuring trick to the social amenities'. Secondly, in recognizing that there was reason enough 'why we should amuse ourselves by collecting Victorian objects of art', he pleaded, like House after him, for discrimination, and he returned to his first distinction. 'Our collector is likely enough to ask us to admire his objects for their aesthetic merit, which, to tell the truth, is far more problematical.' I agree, provided that the adjective 'problematical' is taken seriously.

Fry makes a further general observation of continuing pertinence, relevant, indeed, to all interpretations of Bloomsbury. 'Whether the difference between the nineteenth and twentieth centuries will in retrospect seem as great in life as they already do in art I cannot guess.' Most of us would discover sharper breaks in the late twentieth century than in the late nineteenth, whatever we think of 1910, when 'human character changed' and when Fry met the Bells. Before the Bells was Ashbee and after the Post-Impressionist Exhibitions was Omega. There were nineteenth-century traditions here. Moreover, it is Quentin Bell from the heart of Bloomsbury who has cajoled us more than once into re-examining some of the assumptions about the nineteenth century which at times Fry seems to have taken for granted and who has himself carried out basic historical research. 'I do not think art is as simple as I used to think it,' Fry wrote to Ashbee in 1886. I feel the same in 1986 about history.

DURBINS

Pamela Diamand

IN THE New Year of 1909 we arrived in Guildford in deep snow – my brother Julian and I and our Swiss governess Madeleine – to be conducted to a new house where our father and mother, Roger and Helen Fry, awaited us and where we were all to wait while our very own new house, Durbins, was being built. This rented house was called Chantry Dene and was considered very ugly by Roger, but was exciting for us; it had turrets, and gables and pillared porches, terraces and steps and a summer house in the garden – altogether the opposite of Roger's dignified design for Durbins, but fun to play in. We realized that our mother was not yet her real self. Soon after, she went away; we were never to live with her again.

We enjoyed the snow, which lasted well. Roger took us all to see the field where our house would be built and we tobogganed down the future site of Durbins. One morning at breakfast, he told us that the builders were starting and we were to lay the first bricks. We went off in great excitement and found digging going on and a little bit of wall about two courses up, and the foreman then showed us how to spread the mortar and lay the brick, which I watched very attentively and tried to imitate exactly. However, the bricklayer who was watching laughed and said 'She thinks she's making mud pies', to my great humiliation and disgust. My own grown-ups always observed the common courtesies with us, such as not making remarks about us in front of others.

We were provided with a small can of paint and a brush to inscribe our initials and the date of the ceremony on the bricks, and I suppose they are there to this day.

While we were all at Chantry Dene, a very interesting bearded visitor arrived – he was a stonemason and had come at Roger's behest to carve an inscription on a wooden bridge across the river Wey – which I vaguely feel Roger had something to do with the designing of. This interesting man, whose conversation we listened to intently, was Eric Gill, later to become a famous sculptor. Roger requested him to write out some lines in our copy-books for us to copy. He asked what he should write and Julian said '*Malbrook s'en va't'en guerre*', which was our French song of the moment. So we copied those lines daily, trying our best to imitate the exact writing of Eric Gill.

We were happy at Chantry Dene, as we had both my Aunt Joan's affection and Madeleine's to rely on and we saw Roger. I think it was at Chantry Dene that he made an end-paper for E.M. Forster's *The Celestial Omnibus*. He also spent a good deal of time experimenting with the Japanese technique of painting on silk; I think scenes from Dante; but he was never satisfied, chiefly because he was unhappy and also because he had reached the end of his inspiration from earlier Italian art and had not yet discovered modern art. It lay waiting for him when he was ready.

The excitement grew as the house progressed. The woodwork was all to be treated with creosote, which had just been introduced for interior decoration as the final answer to both cost and maintenance. The fireplaces were all to be constructed of plain fire-resistant bricks, with no grates or other concessions to custom. They were rectangular and tall, with an open hearth tiled red and plain wooden mantels and surrounds. To be quite truthful, they did not give out as much heat as was hoped and many had to be fitted with iron hoods to prevent smoking. However, in the War, we were grateful for the heat given out by the mounds of burning peat in Roger's studio. I understand they are still in use.

This reminds me of a short visit I paid to Charleston at the end of the War. When I arrived, Roger was in a triumphant mood – he had just created a coke-burning stove by himself! He had decided the feeble warmth from the old fireplace must be replaced, and went to Lewes to fetch some fire-brick slabs. He set them up in front of the chimney place to create a stove in the room, bringing the hearth out into the room instead of losing the heat up the chimney. Again, it is still in use.

Heating of Durbins was to be by radiators, as Roger thought the French habit of central heating excellent. The house was of very unusual design – entirely planned by Roger, except the work on the stairway. It consisted of one main hall or living room, the height of two ordinary rooms and the size of more than two rooms in area. Great high windows lit it to the south and sunlight poured in almost all day. A minstrel's gallery on the north wall connected Roger's studio on one side with a dining room on the other. There were plenty of bedrooms tucked into the mansard roof. Roger's studio ran the whole length of the west side. It was lit from three sides; south and west for living and writing and north for painting. The walls were lined with purpose-built drawers to contain his large collection of photographs of works of art from all countries; all neatly labelled in his beautiful clear handwriting (this collection became the nucleus of the Witt photographic library at the Courtauld Institute).

Roger's philosophy for building the house was to select the materials exceedingly carefully, as regards both price and quality, and to standardize wherever possible. For instance, he took great trouble to design the mouldings for the woodwork, but once he was satisfied with them, the same mouldings were used throughout. I think his tastes and preferences naturally favoured the use of the cheaper materials, as he had a positive antipathy to any form of display; and he found interesting effects could be obtained with simple, cheap methods. The Cornish slates he chose had an uneven surface and were a pleasant blue-green grey; considered inferior to the dark Welsh slates he so disliked, and therefore cheaper.

The front elevation was the most remarkable part, its otherwise unbroken flatness relieved by two wide red-brick pilasters positioned either side of the hall. These were flanked by the high windows, reaching nearly to the roof, and the central door was topped by a chequer-board pattern in end-on tiles and white plaster. The shutters framing the four windows at either extremity complete the balance. A little summer house on the right contains an abortive mosaic which I remember was the object of some combined work by Roger and Clive Bell and Duncan Grant one afternoon; but I think they lost patience, as it was hard and trying work and they had better things to do. The legs of the protagonists – badminton players – are still there.

Revisiting it on many occasions, I have been deeply impressed by the fact that all the constructional features of the house, down to the smallest detail, have survived intact through the seventy and more years since it was built; even the radiators are original.

So the house was superb, but it never fulfilled its purpose: my mother was never well enough to come and live there with us. I once said to Roger I had had a wonderful dream that Mummy was well, and he looked so sad as he answered 'I often dream that too' that I never spoke of her again for many years, though we dictated or wrote letters to her every Sunday with Roger in the studio. He never let his grief spoil our lives and fought against it on his own, chiefly with work.

One dark stormy night, a few days before Christmas 1909, we were told the move had taken place, and we went to enter the new house, not as viewers but as its inhabitants. The precious rabbits had been put in our home-made box cart and wheeled to their new home by us in the morning. It was wonderful to go to bed in our own real rooms which we had watched gradually materializing from the very foundations.

The house was built, the rooms were all occupied, and apart from a few small teething troubles the place proved perfectly adapted to our simple style of living. The garden remained to be created. Miss Jekyll, the great pioneer of landscape gardening, lived not far away, and Roger consulted her frequently and obtained complete plans from her, specified in the minutest detail, with every species of plant indicated in her neat drawings.

The garden was designed to take advantage of the slope of the terrain (nobody would have used this word then, except Roger, who always insisted it should be introduced into the English language). It was laid out in a succession of five terraces, the second being flanked by large buttresses constructed from the soil removed to level the lawns and scoop out the ponds, and encased in dry walls made from the local barget stone, where many rock plants were tucked into the crevices to hang out their purple and yellow banners through the glowing summer days. There was a squarish pond and a round one. The square one was peopled with goldfish and water lilies whose island leaves attracted little flocks of linnets and water wagtails. There was also a system of economy in the choice of plants – just one kind of rose, a China rose called a monthly rose for its continued flowering; these were alternated with lavender bushes and grew along the tops of the buttresses, so that they could be seen silhouetted against the skyline. Eric Gill's big statue of a standing woman gazed out on the garden from the centre of the flower border overlooking the pond.

There were herbaceous borders round the fruit cages, and in these grew Roger's favourite oriental poppies, blue anchusa, dropwort, irises and Canterbury bells bordered by white dianthus. The cages themselves were fenced in with espaliered apples and pears. The lowest terrace formed a little-used tennis lawn surrounded by a yew hedge; and right at the end the very prolific vegetable garden, where usual and unusual vegetables grew.

The gravel drive along the west side of the garden was lined with Lombardy poplars and aspens, the breeding ground of cockchafer beetles that buzzed clumsily into our bedrooms on warm summer evenings. With Madeleine's encouragement I learnt to capture them in my hands. She also taught me to catch bumble bees in my cupped hands and hold them there till they squeaked.

Julian and I accepted life as it came, which shows that Roger and Joan's plan for our happy childhood worked well. We were aware of their very differing attitudes to life, Joan seeing it through a profound commitment to Quakerism, to pacifism and vegetarianism, Roger, though at first entrenched in the orthodox art historian's way of life and permanently saddened by our mother's illness, waking up one day to find himself a 'member' (though there never was such a thing) of the Bloomsbury Group (and there never was such a thing as that either!). We naturally became aware of these totally different attitudes co-existing in the house.

In 1910 there was an interruption in our quiet lives of a national character which leaves very vivid memories. I woke up one morning to hear everyone saying that King Edward was dead. My history lessons were limited to most uncompromising lists of 'good' and 'bad' kings, from which I drew the conclusion that we were extremely fortunate to happen to live under a 'good' king and that his successor might easily plunge us all back into the alarming situations prevailing under King John. However, as life went on quietly I was reassured, and all the pageantry of the Proclamation and then the Coronation was most exciting.

Julian was to be a page to Queen Elizabeth, alias our riding mistress, and watching the long procession go by with

Julian in it, even in a steady drizzle, was intensely thrilling; to be followed by bonfires and fireworks for which even our well-ordered timetable was disrupted.

Lunch was always served on the long refectory table in the big hall. With no cloth, polished silver and antique china and glass on the golden oak looked beautiful, and have been permanently celebrated in a spontaneous and delicate still life by Duncan Grant, now in the Fry Room at the Courtauld Institute.

On one winter walk towards the end of the War, I remember Roger picking a bunch of dried silvery calyces and seed boxes of dead flowers. He was looking for something to decorate the hats at the Omega – artificial flowers were usual in hats then – but these were really beautiful. I suspect Roger was once more a bit far ahead of his time – beauty in the unexpected and the unwanted.

Sunday ended with letters to our mother and Roger reading favourite poetry to us – I must not forget that there was usually some Bible lesson with Joan before going to Meeting.

A regular Sunday visitor was E. M. Forster, who came to lunch very often; I think everyone enjoyed his whimsical conversation – also he sat for his portrait, now quite well known, which took a very long time.

Once John Masefield came. His wife was a particular friend of my Aunt Isabel's. He must have found the intellectual conversation as boring as we did, because he left the other guests and came out into the garden with Julian and me and we all sat on a grassy bank and he told us about his flock of guinea-pigs who responded to his whistling and followed him wherever he went. He taught us games with throwing penknives. It was an enchantment. What an approachable man was to become the next Poet Laureate, whereas our cousin Robert Bridges was altogether formidable.

A most colourful occasional visitor was Lady Ottoline Morrell, with her husband. She wore long earrings and a long black velvet hat that dropped down behind like a pirate's cap – most fascinating – and long tight skirts, the hobble skirt being just in fashion. She spoke with a drawl – and I think asked Joan many questions about Quakerism, as she asked to come to Meeting with us on Sunday. She had been very kind to my mother during some of her illnesses.

'Us children' consisted of just Julian and me, but before long Julian was sent to a local prep school, and later to Bedales, and my solitude was relieved by the importation of 'suitable' little girls. They were not my choice, but I played with them and usually let myself be bossed by them. Julia Strachey, who came for about a year, was very much cleverer than I and a great dare-devil. She climbed all the way round the house leaning on the very slightly sloping mansard roof and supported solely by the guttering. I was bullied into doing a small stretch of this exercise, which terrified me. I think Julia did not know what physical fear was and, as I have a full normal quota of it, combined with the moral cowardice which made me even more afraid of being called a 'funk', I gave in to her incitements to risk life and limb and got into many other scrapes which I didn't at all enjoy. She would insist on our sitting on a very narrow ledge at roof height, with our legs dangling into space, playing with the dolls. Again my face was saved by grown-up intervention when 'Aunty Loo', as Alys Bertrand Russell was called, came to visit Julia and said 'No more of that'; but Joan never intervened – such was her faith. I liked Aunty Loo; she was kind and expansive and generous to many children, as she had none of her own.

About 1911, a man called Joseph Wickstead, who had connections with Letchworth School, started up a very small school at a village called Chilworth nearby, and Julian, I think, became a boarder, while Julia Strachey and I went twice a week. I was overjoyed at going to a real school at last, but I record this because Joseph Wickstead read *Hamlet* all through to us and went into the study of the play in detail, and I think that was one of the greatest gifts anyone gave me at the age of nine.

Also we were all taken to London to see the Second Post-Impressionist Exhibition – organized by my father and, as is well known, the subject of a great outcry amongst the *élite* and the not so *élite*. Julia and I were thrilled, especially by the Matisse dancers; we grasped at the liberation, both in terms of subject – nudes dancing seemed so poetical – and freedom of colours and execution. We went home and painted green dancers and mermaids, and Julian an elephant, on the walls in the schoolroom. I only wish I now had all the black and white posters of the exhibition we were then given to enjoy ourselves colouring.

Some time in the summer of 1910, some very different visitors had arrived: Mr and Mrs Bell. They were to become frequent guests and to bring others. Whereas other visitors treated Joan, Roger's own sister, with the usual civilities due to a hostess, these people, who more or less invaded the house, treated Joan with scant consideration. It was evident, even to us children, that she felt uncomfortable and disapproved; they rarely talked to her, and indeed she would not have been interested in their ideas or in Clive's jokes and loud laughter.

Anxious to keep the only home we knew going, Joan bore it. Maybe she saw how much happier Roger was with these new friends and the new interests (like the Post-Impressionist Exhibitions) that he shared with them.

They came for weekends, bringing Duncan Grant with his beguiling smile. They played badminton on the terrace. Once we all played cricket on the tennis lawn. Once Roger, Clive and Duncan set about constructing the mosaic of badminton players that was to embellish the summer house; but it remains today where they left it, at hip length from the ground up. They might be talking, talking endlessly, punctuated by the bass bellowing of Clive's laughter.

A much more successful effort was the painting of 'frescoes' in size colours on the alcove walls of the entrance hall – above the big hall on the ground floor. Three over-life-size nudes took shape there, of which only Duncan's stylized red man was really successful – Vanessa's yellow man was so relaxed he looked rather like a prehistoric ancestor, with his long dangling arms, and Roger's nude with blue hair was more conventional in other ways. They still stand there gazing at anyone who comes into the front hall.

Children are very conservative; I think we enjoyed some of the fun, but not all – Clive's overtures sometimes ended in too much teasing and too much tickling. But I must have felt friendly towards him because I remember writing to tell him I had fallen into the small round pond. Later, in my teens, I sensed something unusual in Roger's attitude to Vanessa; vaguely, uncomfortably I felt that he loved her. She, on her side, may have felt jealous; Roger's deep affection for me was so open and generous, she probably felt I was a barrier. She was the only person to tick me off, which I resented. Later we became quite friendly.

As well as the Bells and their friends, some newly-weds visited us. These were Leonard and Virginia Woolf on one occasion and, another time, Adrian Stephen and Karin, all of whom we knew quite well already. Perhaps their visits stand out in my memory because Roger's more ageing circle was unused to marriages.

We all noticed that Roger's painting was changing. Outlines were becoming assertive and often of a bright colour, shapes were getting blockish, much struggling and over-painting were going on and colours became stronger. I liked some of this, but I never lost my love of some of his sensitive water-colours. During our holiday in Studland, when the Bells were nearby and he and Vanessa struggled with large blocked landscapes, he also did some straight sketches in complete contrast. Back at home he showed me a small, very delicate sketch of the Dorset landscape with an overcast sky which I liked so much that he gave it to me on the spot, though I was only nine. It is still mine, and looks down on me as I write these words; and when I revisited Dorset after very many years I kept seeing this little picture all around me. He had captured the spirit of that corner of England completely.

As well as new visitors there were new pictures and objects. Many pictures came from the Second Post-Impressionist Exhibition. These replaced a number of primitive saints on gold backgrounds, only one of which Roger kept. The newcomers (not in chronological order) were a Picasso abstract which I cannot describe, a still life of bananas and pears in a flower pot, which I still enjoy, by Marchand – a very quiet, balanced picture – and another Marchand of bathers under a tree, slightly cubist but well-balanced figures in a calm landscape (now at Rodwell House). Also two or three Lhotes and a Villette, as well as the large painting by Thiesson. About this time, Roger bought the Brancusi head of Mlle Pogani, in bronze. That and his beautiful Chinese Kwan Yin statue stood on either side of the hall stairway, on rough-hewn oak plinths. He also bought a beautiful screen of a phoenix on a silver-gilt background. The head of a beautiful, mysterious and evocative girl by Doucet also joined the collection.

The summer of 1911 was especially lovely and very hot. We came out with German measles at the height of the heatwave, the only compensation being the beautiful and loving way in which Joan nursed us. No sooner was this over for me, and Julian become the patient, than Vanessa and Henri Doucet arrived to paint my portrait. Roger had bought his head of a young girl, and I always believe he hoped that Doucet would do something equally beautiful of me, completely lacking as I was in the poise and mysterious beauty of his *jeune fille*.

The paints and canvases were being assembled by the pond, but Duncan Grant, who was to be of the party – and I suspect that the plan may have partly been devised to help him financially – did not arrive. One day, two days went by and to everyone's consternation Duncan still did not arrive. Finally, in the evening of the second day, we heard his footsteps coming up the drive. Everyone exclaimed 'Duncan, where *have* you been?' Oh, said Duncan in his innocent way, he had not been able to find the one shilling and sixpence to pay for the train fare to Guildford. Finally he said 'I had a nightmare, or rather a day mare, that I had left a florin at the back of a drawer, and I found it and so I came.'

In the meantime sittings had taken place. I had been given the choice of pose, and had sat down at random by the big pond, with my legs out straight in front of me, parallel to the edge of the pond. No one realized at the time that this was a most tiring position to hold. I was held responsible for the failure of all the paintings save Duncan's because I could not go on smiling, to the exasperation of Doucet – 'Ah!,' he would constantly exclaim, '*elle ne sourit plus.*' Duncan wisely seized an opportunity during a rest, and his quite natural and girlish portrait survives as a good picture today – but it was a long, long time till I could bring myself to admit to its very real qualities.

On a hot July day in 1913, Joy Brown was entrusted to take Julian and me to London for a very special occasion – the opening of the Omega Workshops. I think we had lunch at 41 Gordon Square with the Bells and went with Julian and Quentin (in prams) on foot to the Marylebone Baths, but, as I had developed one of those devastating sore throats of childhood, all that part of the day, which was no doubt supposed to amuse us, is clouded in misery. But I remember clearly being taken into the front room of 33 Fitzroy Square, where there were all these brilliant coloured hangings and screens which I couldn't now remember individually and which have probably coalesced in my memory with the photographic images taken on that day.

One other memory connected with the Omega remains very vivid. Our Swiss governess Madeleine, who had returned, while Joy Brown joined the staff of the Omega as dress-maker, took me on a grey autumn day to Mitcham, where the pottery then used by the Omega was. The whole place impressed itself so clearly on my memory that when, over sixty years later and happening to be on a bus, not knowing it would go through Mitcham, I looked out and saw a 'green' I knew I had seen it before and that it must be Mitcham – I had never been back. The pottery was a huge barn of a place, with pots drying all round the walls. In one central area was the magic wheel; I don't remember clearly what mechanism powered it, probably a large fly-wheel. Roger was at work making lumps of clay into real shapes. (Having studied pottery a little since, I now know they were the kind of shapes students are obliged to scrap, but then they were thrilling!)

Roger's original intention had been to train the commercial potter who owned the place, a nice strong-looking man with a grizzled beard, but when it came to the point he could only repeat the shapes his hands were trained to make repetitively all day. Roger, sensing the possibilities of this wonderfully creative medium, rolled up his sleeves and plunged into the craft of pottery forthwith. Certainly his first pots were clumsy and would not have passed at art school, but gradually he acquired great skill. Always he was guided by his strong sense of form, with a leaning towards the Chinese. Mitcham Pottery provided a beautiful turquoise glaze with accidental flecks of colour from other glazes here and there; also a rather unpleasant pea-green. I was allowed to have a try and produced two little embryonic pots, the thrill of which remained with me all my life and eventually impelled me to try making pottery on my own.

Later on, during school holidays, Roger took me on one of his weekend pottery expeditions to the Poole Pottery. It was wartime and trains and lodgings were all more difficult, but such things never deterred him. It seems to me the pottery was somewhere along the waterfront. On the Saturday we were met by Mr Caster, the manager, who arranged for the girls to be there to provide the ready wedged clay and turn the great fly-wheel. He pointed out that the old man in the corner would remain at work all the weekend because he was so unhappy away from the pottery. His work was the finishing of the large clay figures which used to be displayed in the windows of dairies. I was always fascinated by them, large sleek cows, pretty dairy-maids, farmers in smocks. The thought of them today brings back the cool smell of large bowls of milk.

SICKERT AND BLOOMSBURY

Martin Gayford

'WHAT DO you think of Sickert's painting?', Virginia Woolf enquired of Quentin Bell in November 1933. 'I gather Roger is rather down on it; so is Clive. It seems to me all that painting ought to be. Am I wrong? If so why?' Her musings anticipate the foray into the territory of art criticism which emerged the following year as *Walter Sickert: A Conversation*. But she also raised an interesting question. Was it really true that the Bloomsbury critics were 'rather down' on the work of Walter Sickert, a man widely regarded as the greatest English painter of his day? If so, were they right? And why?

There were, of course, important artistic issues at stake between Fry and Bell on one side and Sickert on the other. First, they divided – in rather knockabout fashion – as to the relative importance of form and content (a venerable aesthetic conundrum). About this there was at times absurd absolutism on both sides: the Bloomsbury critics notoriously championing formal values – 'significant form', in Clive Bell's phrase. 'It's all the same to me if I represent a Christ or a saucepan', Fry once remarked, and Quentin Bell heard him refer to the agonized body of Christ on the cross as 'this important mass'. Sickert in reaction proclaimed that 'all great art is illustration, illustration, illustration all the time.' 'I have always been a literary painter, thank goodness, like all the decent painters', he informed Virginia Woolf. 'Do be the first to say so.' (In fact she didn't, quite, as will appear below.)

Beneath this dispute there were other factors at work. One of these was certainly the Post-Impressionist Exhibition of 1910, by which Sickert had good reason to feel upstaged. Previously he, Sickert, had been the elder statesman of the artistic *avant-garde* in Britain; now he found radical painters from abroad – men like Matisse and Cézanne, about whom he was dubious himself – presented as the shape of art to come. And this was done, furthermore, by a younger man (Sickert was born in 1860, Fry in 1866), an ex-pupil of his, about whose own work he was not enthusiastic, a fellow who for years had been engaged in the harmless connoisseurship of those boring early Italian painters whose names all end in 'ini' and 'ucci'. It was really very provoking, and hard to respond to.

Sickert reviewed the exhibition cautiously, praising Gauguin and, grudgingly, Van Gogh, but affecting to regard Cézanne – in the eyes of Fry and Bell the greatest figure of all – as a touching but sadly simple-minded uncle of Impressionism. When Clive Bell's *Art* came out in 1914, containing high praise for Cézanne ('the type of the perfect artist'), Sickert observed tartly that in the presence of such statements the reader asks himself 'whether it is the writer or himself who is what my friend Hubby calls "roofy"'.

In return, Fry had reservations about Sickert's friend, mentor and greatest influence, Degas, which led to the following sharp exchange:

Fry: 'It took Degas 40 years to get rid of his cleverness.'

Sickert: 'And it will take you 80 years to get it.'

Furthermore, Fry – otherwise a man of wide aesthetic sympathies – found the painting of his native land deeply uncongenial. With the exception of Constable, he thought the English a 'minor school' – 'linear, descriptive and non-plastic', and Victorian art worse than that, 'sunk to a level of trivial ineptitude'. Once again, unsurprisingly, we find Sickert taking the opposite line, glorying in the prosy novelistic work of painters like Frith and Landseer, and keeping a particularly ripe example in his studio '*pour emmerder* Roger Fry'.

Fry and Bell, indeed, seem to have become an *idée fixe* with Sickert. 'Great jokes about Roger', Virginia noted of her meeting with Sickert in December 1933, 'Oh Roger's a darling, but dear me . . .' Jokes about Fry there were in profusion, but the preoccupation seems to have run deep. 'Is that Roger?', Quentin Bell reports the aged Sickert enquiring at a lecture some years after Fry's death. 'And from this rather disquieting remark', Bell adds, 'I judge that Sickert could not rid his mind of his old opponent.'

Nor it seemed, could Clive Bell, whose memoir of Sickert, written after the painter's death, reveals persisting irritation.

'The opinions of Walter Sickert,' he snorted, 'what were they? They boxed the compass between a first and a third glass of wine.' And, further, 'In no sense was Sickert a scholar; for if his acquaintance with books was scrappy, his acquaintance with pictures was not much better.' All of which may well have been true, although one could fairly add that the erudition of a painter needs to be of a very different sort from that required by an art critic or a professor.

Sickert's talk and writing were laced with mischievous fun. The underlying assumption was that truths were more likely to be uncovered by the swift and witty overturning of platitudes than by slow and solemn discussion. He belonged to an era – the Wildean, Whistlerian Eighties and Nineties – that regarded conversation as an art form, and also a sport – somewhat akin to fencing. It was also a milieu that valued the mask, and appreciated the dandified pose – which may help us understand why the painter so loved to change his appearance: grow beards, shave them off, dress as a tramp, a lord, a cook. And, similarly, why he loved to strike an attitude when writing or speaking – this line would sound good, and, who knows, it might be right. Of course, he was also, unquestionably, a bit of a ham. But none of this – as Quentin Bell has pointed out – prevented an essential seriousness about his art, nor a fundamental consistency in the doctrines he propounded.

However, this playful spirit grated on serious, Cantabrigian Bloomsbury. 'He was a *poseur* by choice; he was naughty by nature and he never ceased to be an actor', growled Clive Bell. 'I wish', Fry wrote in 1925, 'he were not so anxious to pretend that this business of art is all a joke.' 'But', Fry added wearily, 'everything about Walter Sickert has to have the same air of paradox.'

In the circumstances it is a little surprising that friendly relations between Sickert and the Bloomsbury critics persisted, but they did. For one thing – somewhat contrary to Virginia Woolf's assumption – both Bloomsbury critics praised and collected Sickert's own work. Clive Bell wrote that his own admiration was 'I hope, fairly well-known' (and surmised it was the reason why Sickert 'did me the honour of treating me as a friend'). But, though Bell thought Sickert the greatest English painter since Constable, he thought he had talent, not genius – he wasn't up to the best of the French. Fry – believing that at any one time the leading British painter was no better than a good Frenchman in the second division – doubtless concurred. Nonetheless a Sickert was in pride of place over the mantelpiece in Fry's house at 7 Dalmeny Avenue. Clive Bell recorded how he acquired a 'little masterpiece' of a Sickert drawing for £5, the artist having originally presented it to him gratis on the ground that Bell 'knew and admired the model', and, in Sickert's view, 'when a man's had a lech on a girl he has a right to her picture'. In his memoir of Sickert (to which I am much indebted) Quentin Bell has painted an unforgettable picture of the painter and his father, meeting by chance in a Soho restaurant in the Twenties, and, 'both slightly fuddled, singing together such music hall songs as "Daisy, Daisy" and "The Duke of Clarence has passed away . . . Ta-rar-rar-rar-ra *boom* de-ay"'.

Such conviviality does not seem to have existed between Sickert and Fry – the relish for the music hall was one of many Sickertian tastes Fry found incomprehensible – but theirs was a long friendship, and, in a way, a deep one. At one stage Fry stayed with the Sickert family in Dieppe, and in 1893 he attended evening classes run by Sickert at The Vale, Chelsea. But in the long run, as Marjorie Lilly observed, 'painting, which should have forged a link between them . . . merely drove them apart'. Sickert's admiration for Fry's own paintings – like posterity's – seems to have been lukewarm, although sometimes in print he praised them. His enthusiasm for Fry's lectures, however, was unfeigned. Not only did he attend them, he was to be found in the front row, applauding vigorously. 'No sooner', he explained, 'do I see the feet of Mr Roger Fry on the mountains than I scamper, bleating, to sit at them.' It was of Fry the lecturer that Sickert produced his memorable etching 'Vision, Volumes and Recession' – a caricature, perhaps, but an affectionate one.

It is a wonder that the two men maintained even moderately amicable relations; they were almost comically dissimilar. Fry was in origin, as Clive Bell wrote, 'lofty and puritan', the offspring of legal sagacity and industrious Quaker chocolate manufacture; Sickert was the son of an unsuccessful Danish painter and the illegitimate daughter of a Cambridge don and an Irish dancer. Fry went to King's, was grounded in Natural Sciences and became an Apostle. He was a scholar. Sickert toyed with acting, then learnt his art from Whistler and Degas. He was a man of the world.

Just as Sickert's mountebank habits and Yellow Book manner annoyed Fry, Fry's intellectualizing and White Knight unpracticality jarred on Sickert – Mr Fry, he wrote, 'seems to me to drop occasionally into Double-Dutch, only to be understood by those having a Super-University education'. Nina Hamnett, perhaps mistress of both, once confided in Quentin Bell that 'The difference between Roger and Walter was this: Walter knew I was a bitch; Roger, bless his heart, never did.'

'You and I', Fry once summed up the position to Sickert, 'both live in the firm belief that one of us is destined to do the other in, and, that being the only thing that keeps both of us alive, we should not do it as we should both have lost our motive for living.'

Between Fry and Sickert, I suspect, deeper than the clash of ideas and temperaments, there was a difference of ideals. It was not only that they disagreed about form and content, English and French art, they were moved by different things. Fry was the kind of Englishman who finds his native land, that 'Bird's Custard Island', unappealing to the point of physical repulsion. For him, the place of the heart was the south, Provence, the land of Cézanne – a terrain of lucidity, austerity and sculptural fullness. This formal order satisfied him deeply – for Fry this cerebral harmony was a sort of content. Sickert, on the contrary, cosmopolitan though he was, found his most intense inspiration in seedy north London bed-sits where the very wallpaper seemed impregnated with the haphazard drama of everyday life.

Here, of course, neither man was right, neither wrong. Now we see that Fry and Bell were entirely correct in their estimation of Cézanne and Matisse. Both were greater than any painter at work in Britain; greater than Sickert. But Sickert was right, also, to pursue his muse regardless. It is not enough in art to follow the best models, as the classicists of the academies showed through centuries of hapless attempts to emulate Raphael. Sickert, like every true artist, had his own individual constitution, and his personal patch of material to cultivate. Fry and the Post-Impressionists, of course, in the long run had a tremendous impact on the art of Britain. But we still have today – in Lucian Freud and Leon Kossoff, for example – important painters who excavate that Sickertian vein of London dinginess.

About the question of form v. content, it seems to me that Virginia Woolf took a wiser course than either painter or critic. Her essay, significantly, is not called *Walter Sickert: A Dissertation* but *Walter Sickert: A Conversation*. It is a discussion in which the claims of literary content and those of the silent language of colour and design are alternately advanced. At points in the discussion the literary interpretation of the painter's work is pushed very far, so that in a picture like 'Ennui' – two lethargic figures in a shabby room – both a social vignette and a comment on the human condition are found. In 'Ennui', one speaker remarks, the grimness 'lies in the fact that there is no crisis; dull minutes are mounting, old matches are accumulating and dirty glasses and dead cigars; still on they must go, up they must get'. And yet, says the other speaker, it is beautiful, 'Perhaps it is the flash of the stuffed birds in the case, or the relation of the chest of drawers to the woman's body; anyhow, there is a quality in that picture which makes me feel that . . . still in the other world . . . beauty and order prevail.'

This surely is the only line to take. On the one hand, perhaps there is no great art without emotional, literary, political or other human meaning. On the other, it cannot be the content that makes it art – otherwise there would be no distinction between painting and essays or propaganda. It is the *fusion* of this content with form and colour which counts; and on the nature of that fusion even the most eloquent criticism begins to falter. 'We have reached the edge where painting breaks off and takes her way into the silent land . . . and all our words will fold their wings and sit huddled like rooks on the tops of trees in winter.'

2
VIRGINIA AND VANESSA

TWO SISTERS: VIRGINIA WOOLF AND VANESSA BELL

Lyndall Gordon

IN JULY 1897 Stella, the eldest sister in the motherless Stephen household, died. In September Virginia, the youngest sister, wrote in the first of all her diaries that life was 'lengthening indeed but death would be shorter and less painful'. At fifteen she needed some answer to the cruelty of fate and this her elder sister, Vanessa, gave her: 'Nessa preaches that our destiny lies in ourselves . . .'

At this stage the three men in the household began to prey on the sisters in different ways: their father, Leslie Stephen, became more tyrannical; their bereaved brother-in-law, Jack Hills, exacted minute analysis of his grief; and their half-brother, George, caught them in rather too passionate embraces which he represented, even to himself, as overmastering brotherly affection. The two young women could exert no control, but they 'walked alone' whenever they could. At 22 Hyde Park Gate they found privacy in a glass-enclosed room overlooking the back garden. There Vanessa would paint while Virginia read aloud from Thackeray and George Eliot. It was then, said Virginia, that 'Nessa and I formed together a very close conspiracy. In that world of many men, coming and going, we formed our private nucleus.'

Virginia Stephen's diary-essays of 1903 and her diary of 1904–5 help to explain the conditions that made home intolerable and how drastically, in the sisters' eyes, they were changed by their move to Bloomsbury. October 1904 marked the beginning of a new life. Virginia Stephen, aged twenty-two, no longer had to look out on Mrs Redgrave washing her neck across a narrow street. She looked out on trees which seemed to fountain up in the middle of Gordon Square. More important, she now had a separate work-room with a very high desk where she would stand to write for two and a half hours each morning.

She stood, she claimed, to be even with Vanessa who complained of standing for hours at an easel, but the posture may have suited the seething energy that she inherited from her father.

The sisters now planned their day around work, and their bonding – which had once been a conspiratorial necessity – became now a fertile basis both for their experiments in art and for their new group, giving that group its domestic character as their brother's friends shifted from Cambridge into a feminized setting dominated by two original and determined women.

Of the sisters Vanessa was the more overtly daring. She flaunted bawdy talk and, at a party in 1911, shook off all her upper clothing as she danced. She declared to Sydney Waterlow that she wanted to form a circle on the principle of complete sexual freedom.

Virginia appeared to follow. When Vanessa took a lover, Roger Fry, in 1911, Virginia bathed naked with Rupert Brooke in the river at Grantchester. That year Virginia set up house with a number of bachelors (including Leonard Woolf) at 34 Brunswick Square and, when George Duckworth protested its impropriety, Vanessa retorted coolly, on her sister's behalf, that the Foundling Hospital was handy. The sisters had African dresses made of printed cotton. They dressed themselves as Gauguin pictures and careered around Crosby Hall at a ball to mark the end of the Second Post-Impressionist Exhibition in 1912. But, as the years passed, it became obvious that this flaunting rebellion did not wholly engage Virginia, who proved more concerned with mental than sexual freedom.

'Do you think we have the same pair of eyes, only different spectacles?', Virginia once asked her sister. There are paintings of women where Vanessa Bell shares the novelist's eye with extraordinary exactitude. Writing of Vanessa Bell's 'Portrait of a Lady' (1912), Richard Shone remarked 'a certain unemphatic air of mystery'. But this is no beguiling Mona Lisa whose mystery is spurious, part of her equipment. The mystery comes partly from a face shadowed by ornamental hair and partly from the unguarded expressionlessness, as though the artist has caught the woman in a moment of unstudied repose just as Virginia Woolf was to catch Mrs Ramsay as the beam of the lighthouse hits her. The eyes of Vanessa Bell's Lady are unseeing. Her mouth is unsmiling – not sad, not inviting, not composed in any communicative act. The mystery lies in the firmly closed lips, the inward-looking eyes, the slight hunch of the body, a picture of muted intelligence which is perfectly complemented by Virginia Woolf's characters, Mrs Ramsay and Isa Oliver. Both sisters play up the gap between silent, placid, decorous conduct and inward mental action.

Vanessa Bell's faceless portraits of Virginia Woolf provide an inspired comment on her hidden nature in contrast with the exquisitely lifeless beauty photographed by Beresford in 1903 or the sharp, insistent image-making of Man Ray who, in the 1920s, photographed Virginia Woolf as an advanced Modern.

Within the charmed circle of Bloomsbury and at Charleston, Vanessa Bell presided, painting or sewing in her impregnable pool of calm, and round her the sister darted, Angelica Garnett recalls, 'like the dragon-fly round the waterlily'. Ottoline Morrell saw Vanessa's character 'like a broad river, not worried or sensitive to passers-by. She carries along the few barques that float with her on her stream of life, her two sons and daughter, but the sea towards which she flows is her painting, above all the thing which is of importance to her.' Virginia, as novelist, was more drawn to passers-by, ranging more widely in both the society and street life of London. When Sydney Waterlow dined with the sisters in December 1910 he noted this essential difference: 'Vanessa icy, cynical, artistic; Virginia much more emotional and interested in life rather than beauty'.

Their temperamental difference may have stimulated their reciprocity. For they were, in a subtle way yet to be defined, co-workers.* And if the sisters were indeed the fountain of Bloomsbury, it is fitting that it was Vanessa Bell who finally painted the group's portrait, just as her sister finally immortalized the group in *The Waves*.**

* Since this was first published, Jane Dunn has explored this subject in *A Very Close Conspiracy: Vanessa Bell and Virginia Woolf* (London: Cape, 1990).

** This article, first published in the *Charleston Newsletter*, was derived largely from *Virginia Woolf: A Writer's Life* by Lyndall Gordon, 1984, by permission of Oxford University Press.

LESLIE STEPHEN AND VIRGINIA WOOLF

Alan Bell

THE GAUNT features of Sir Leslie Stephen, known from G.F. Watts's sensitive portrait or from the studio photographs of his sad and deaf old age, are memorable and haunting. So too is the memory of his domestic character as the domineering father of Vanessa Bell and Virginia Woolf, with his demanding Hebraic lamentations ringing painfully through his intimate autobiography *The Mausoleum Book*. And so too the partial portrait of him as Mr Ramsay in *To the Lighthouse* is one of his daughter's most memorable fictional characters. He is saddled with a personal reputation far worse than he deserves, for against the domestic tyrant we have to set the friend rightly esteemed by so many discerning contemporaries, the intrepid pioneering Alpinist, the super-industrious Victorian man of letters – critic, editor, biographer, essayist – and perhaps above all the courageous secularist. His failings at home, obvious but understandable, are all too well known; at the same time, the achievements of his public career should not be forgotten.

Noël Annan's *Leslie Stephen: the Godless Victorian* (1984), a substantially revised edition of the biographical study first published in 1951, ranges widely from its biographical base to make excursions into the intellectual history of Victorian England, still retaining much of the freshness of the Cambridge prize essay on which the first edition was based. It draws for its fresh biographical material on documents newly available in the British Library, which are also printed fully in the revised and enlarged edition, assembled by Jeanne Schulkind, of *Virginia Woolf: Moments of Being* (1985), in which pages 107–125 are added to help us reassess Virginia Woolf's changing attitude to her father. The full publication of Stephen's *The Mausoleum Book* (1977) had earlier shown Stephen's mourning after the sudden death of his second wife in a more sympathetic light, and in 1985, the centenary year of the first volume of the *Dictionary of National Biography*, his achievements as an editor have not gone unnoticed.

Moments of Being, even in its first edition one of the most valuable products of the Bloomsbury industry, now presents in full both of Virginia Woolf's contrasting memoirs of her father. The first, a relatively early literary exercise, is the *Reminiscences* of 1907, in which she adopts the rather judicial tone of an obituarist writing a time-capsule for her infant nephew Julian. She is sad about her mother, angry (in a way Vanessa never ceased to be) about her father, a man with 'much of the stuff of a Hebrew prophet'. The vehemence of her feelings about his demands on Vanessa and Stella is scarcely mitigated by respect for his literary achievement and influence; writing for Vanessa's family, she partakes all the more of her sister's sustained resentment of Leslie Stephen's domestic exigencies.

Yet in *A Sketch of the Past*, of 1939, she is able to give a much more balanced view of her father. 'I was thinking of my two memoirs,' she wrote in 1940. 'How I see father from the 2 angles. As a child condemning; as a woman of 58 understanding – I shd say tolerating. Both views true? . . .' The tone of this later essay is more intimate; assured but still experimental in manner, it does not merely bask in reminiscence but tries at the same time to explore the byways of memory. The tactile, auditory values of the nursery come out well, not least the silence of Hyde Park Gate after Julia Stephen's death, when the noises of childhood were suddenly cut off by the bereavement.

By 1939 Virginia Woolf was able to recognize how great a psychological discharge writing *To the Lighthouse* had been. She recalled how up to her forties the presence of her mother had obsessed her, rather unhealthily, until the new book was conceived 'in a great, apparently involuntary rush', while walking round Tavistock Square; after it was written, quickly and efficiently, she ceased to be obsessed by her mother and was able to start to reassess her father. 'Just as I rubbed out a good deal of the force of my mother's memory by writing about her in *To the Lighthouse*,' she wrote in 1939, 'so I rubbed out much of his memory there too. Yet he too obsessed me for years. Until I wrote it out, I would find my lips moving; I would be arguing with him; saying to myself all that I never said to him. How deep they drove themselves into me, the things it was impossible to say aloud.'

To the Lighthouse, for all its therapeutic effect, is of course fictional rather than autobiographical, and to make too neat a parallel between Mr and Mrs Ramsay and Mr and Mrs Stephen, to speak of the 'transcription' of experience, is too commonplace a notion for Virginia Woolf's creative interpretation of her past. 'I did not mean to paint an exact portrait of my father in Mr Ramsay,' she wrote to Jacques-Émile Blanche in 1927, 'a book makes everything into itself, and the portrait became changed to fit it as I wrote.' Nevertheless a great deal of Mr Ramsay/Stephen's personality does come over, not least in the frustrations of a man of limited genius not able to advance beyond Q in the alphabetical scale of intellectual achievement, his sense of the 'good second class' mind leading to despondency, self-centredness and brooding on failure.

The change in her feelings for him is suggested by a diary entry of 1928, on what would have been Leslie Stephen's ninety-sixth birthday. 'He would have been . . . 96; but mercifully was not. His life would have entirely ended mine. What would have happened? No writing, no books; – inconceivable.' After *To the Lighthouse*, 'He comes back now more as a contemporary. I must read him some day. I wonder if I can feel again, I hear his voice . . .' An opportunity for reappraisal had come at Leslie Stephen's centenary in 1932, with an invitation to write a commemorative article for *The Times*, through which she could show herself, and the world, that the portrait of Mr Ramsay was not intended to be the whole story. She could write appreciatively there of his physical characteristics and energy, his intellectual attitudes, even of his endless worries about money: all is done with more balance than hitherto, and with perceptive humour. She could also publicly declare her own literary debt to him, especially for allowing his fifteen-year-old daughter the free run of his own shelves, supplemented by armfuls of books brought home for her from the London Library.

> To read what one liked because one liked it, never to pretend to admire what one did not – that was his only lesson in the art of reading. To write in the fewest possible words, as clearly as possible – that was his only lesson in the art of writing. Yet a child must have been childish in the extreme not to feel that such was the teaching of a man of great learning and wide experience, though he would never impose his own views or parade his own knowledge.

And so the intolerable aspects of his private life are muted in a more tolerant recognition of his public achievement, as if a preparation for the more affectionate *Sketch of the Past* of 1939, which is now at last fully available to show what she felt of the years in which 'Nessa and I were fully exposed without protection to the full blast of that strange character'.

ROGER FRY AND VIRGINIA WOOLF: PICTURES AND BOOKS

Jacky Thompson

'So roger appeared', wrote Virginia Woolf in her sketch of the origins of Bloomsbury presented to the Memoir Club around 1922.

> He appeared, I seem to think, in a large ulster coat every pocket of which was stuffed with a book, a paint box, or something intriguing; he had canvasses under his arms; his hair flew; his eyes glowed. He had more knowledge and experience than the rest of us put together. And at once we were all launched into a terrific argument about literature; we had down Milton; we re-read Wordsworth. We had to think the whole thing over again. The old skeleton arguments of primitive Bloomsbury about art and beauty put on flesh and blood. There was always some new idea afoot; always some new picture standing on a chair to be looked at, some new poet fished out from obscurity and stood in the light of day.

The meeting that was to bring this new life and energy into the group happened by chance in the spring of 1910 on a train travelling from Cambridge to London. The occupants of the carriage were Roger Fry and a young married couple, Clive and Vanessa Bell. 'We fell into talk about contemporary art and its relation to all other art', says Clive Bell in the introduction to *Art*, his work on aesthetic theory; 'it seems to me sometimes that we have been talking about the same thing ever since'. The subject was already central to each of their lives. Vanessa Bell was practising her vocation as a painter, and Clive as an amateur of aesthetics. Roger Fry, having turned his back on the comfort and respectability of his established position in the art world, was just planning a project that was to turn him for a long while into its demon king. In November that same year his exhibition 'Manet and the Post-Impressionists' opened at the Grafton Gallery in London, and gave the British public its first outraged look at the works of Cézanne, Van Gogh, Matisse, Picasso and those painters who since the 1870s had revolutionized European art.

To a whole group of young English painters, among them Vanessa Bell, the exhibition was a revelation, and they at once adopted Roger Fry as their guide to this new world he had opened for them. On Virginia Woolf his influence grew more slowly. Years later, she chose to date the beginning of the whole modern era from the Exhibition when she wrote in her essay on the genesis of the modern novel, 'Mr Bennett and Mrs Brown', 'On or about December 1910 human nature changed.' At the time, though, she paid it only cursory attention, and found *him*, sixteen years her elder, a distinguished and formidable figure. It was through the love they shared for her sister Vanessa that she first began to draw close to him. Perhaps she understood in him the same feelings of hurt and bafflement she also experienced at being held at a distance by Vanessa. 'Roger and I had a frog's chorus such as you might have heard at Charleston,' she wrote to her in 1918, 'but you'd only have asked Duncan to shut the window if you had. You can imagine the dismal croaks – how we loved and sung and despaired.' It was the desire to penetrate her sister's life as much as the lure of Roger's fiery enthusiasm that led her at about this time to embark on a course of self-education in art. There were visits to art galleries, where under Roger's professorial eye she had to confess to liking all the wrong paintings for the wrong reasons. There were actual purchases from the latest shows. But above all, inevitably, there was talk. 'I don't see how to put 3 or 4 hours of Roger's conversation into the rest of this page', complains her diary. And in 1917 she records a discussion between Roger and Clive Bell on literature and aesthetics with her in the supporting role of eager novice: 'Roger asked me if I founded my writing upon texture or structure; I connected structure with plot, and therefore said "texture". Then we discussed the meaning of structure and texture in painting and writing . . .'

Thus she was led by Roger Fry into that most seductive corner of the world of aesthetic theory, 'the sunny margin of the forest', as she called it, 'where the arts flirt and joke and pay each other compliments'. Here was his special territory. The translator of Mallarmé, the impassioned painter, the initiator of Virginia Woolf into the works of Proust, the founder of the Omega Workshops, he could press all the arts into the service of the theory of the moment. 'I have been attacking poetry to understand painting', he wrote in 1913 to his friend G.L. Dickinson. And like a good pupil, when later she was trying in her critical essays to formulate her own novel aesthetic, Virginia Woolf often turned to painting to illuminate the problems facing a writer. 'A book fades like a mist, like a dream. How are we to take a stick and point to that tone, that relation, in the vanishing pages, as Mr Roger Fry points with his wand at a line or a colour in the picture displayed before him?'

It is clear from these same essays that Virginia Woolf saw a close identity between the defence of modern writing she undertook in the Twenties and Roger Fry's championship of the young painters of ten years earlier. He was in fact engaged in a battle of ideas to do with the artist's role in society that can be traced back to Plato's *Republic*, but which had taken on a contemporary urgency with the advent, so frightening and apparently hostile to the public at large, of Modernism in the arts. The first, age-old, area of dispute is that of the relationship of art to life. If art is an imitation of reality, must it not aim to represent to us what we all perceive? Equally, must not an artist express through his works the aims and beliefs of his society? The Exhibition had revealed to the public the depth of the gulf that had opened between its assumptions and the preoccupations of contemporary artists. Tolstoy's recent tract 'What is Art?' spoke for many in its slashing attack on what he called the perverse and counterfeit art of the modern movement. Together Fry and Bell mounted a counter-attack on Tolstoy and on these assumptions. Their thesis was that art was akin not to morality but to religion. In painterly terms this means that artists must be free from pressures to reinforce through their work current social or moral doctrines, and to assert instead their own vision. Further, Fry's counter to the claim that the paintings of the Post-Impressionists were not 'lifelike' is that 'these artists do not seek to imitate form, but to create form: they aim not at illusion but at reality'.

So when Virginia Woolf seeks to explain to a reading public

accustomed to the solidly crafted, realistic works of Galsworthy, H.G. Wells and Arnold Bennett the reasons behind the apparently incomprehensible waywardness of the experimental works of James Joyce, D.H. Lawrence, T.S. Eliot and herself, she draws largely on these aesthetic formulations. Her own contribution to the thesis that art is not imitative but creative comes in those famous lines from her essay 'Modern Fiction' in which, after teasing Arnold Bennett and his 'magnificent apparatus for catching life' from which nonetheless the spirit, or reality, seems to have escaped, she describes this life which the novelist must seek to entrap as 'not a series of gig-lamps symmetrically arranged [but] a luminous halo, a semi-transparent envelope surrounding us from the beginning of consciousness to the end'. And she finds the novelist's equivalent to the painter's freedom of vision in a rejection of the established domination of plot, and of 'the general tidying up of the last chapter, the marriage, the death . . . the statement of values so sonorously trumpeted forth' in which nonetheless 'nothing is solved, we feel, nothing is rightly held together'.

Thus in *To the Lighthouse*, that great experimental novel, which is in itself an acting out of the mode by which the artist translates the transient and shifting world of experience into the static and eternal world of art, she chooses to embody this creative processs not in a writer but in a painter, Lily Briscoe, through whose vision the memory of a summer's day is crystallized into a work of art which is both a painting and the book itself. And while the figure of Lily, that solitary observing eye, is at once an act of homage to her sister and a projection into the book of the writer herself, it has surely as much to do with the inspiration, to Virginia Woolf's work as in her life, of her friend and mentor Roger Fry.

A BIOGRAPHER'S DILEMMA: VIRGINIA WOOLF AND ROGER FRY

Mitchell Leaska

'HOW', WROTE Virginia Woolf in despair, 'how can one make a life out of six cardboard boxes full of tailors' bills, love letters and old picture postcards?' How indeed! And yet all of her professional life as an essayist Virginia wrote miniature portraits of people who perhaps had even less to provide her with by way of archival material; and the lives she evoked represent some of her most brilliant writing. Roger Fry's biography, compared with the rest of the canon, however, stands alone. It is of course an entirely competent biography, but stylistically it lacks sweep and lustre. Leonard Woolf was the first to recognize its weakness and didn't hesitate to tell her what he thought. His criticism felt to Virginia 'like being pecked by a very hard beak. The stronger he pecked the deeper . . .' (It is perhaps significant that the image she used here was the very one she had several years earlier applied to Mr Ramsay – that is, to her father, Leslie Stephen.)

The question remains, however: what was behind Virginia's struggle to commemorate Roger's life? We know now from published letters and diaries that 1938, the year she began the actual writing, was for her a time of turmoil and despair. She had just emerged from almost five years of 'sweat and tears' during the writing of *The Years*; her nephew Julian Bell had been killed in the Spanish Civil War; the publication of *Three Guineas* was accompanied by the usual anticipation anxieties. Most important, perhaps, her work on the biography forced her once more, as had *The Years* a little earlier, to plunge into a memory-laden past to assemble the life of a man who over the years had established a private place in her life and whose significance appears not to have become apparent to her until his death. So that by 1939, as she became encased in the labour of fitting together the pieces of Roger Fry's life, the emotional interference, now increasingly apparent, caused her to doubt herself not only as a biographer but as a writer.

During the early period of the writing, she confessed to her diary how appalling the grind had become: (7 July, 1938) 'It's all too minute and tied down . . . I think I will go on doggedly till I meet him myself – 1909 – and then attempt something more fictitious. But must plod on through all those letters till then.' A few weeks later: (17 August, 1938) 'No I won't go on doing Roger-abstracting with blood and sweat . . .' What Virginia seems not to have anticipated at the time of these entries was that, when she finally did meet (now on paper) Roger again in 1909, she would soon be seeing him as Vanessa's lover.

By 1909 Vanessa had become the closest person in Virginia's life; and, more than a sister, Vanessa had become in many significant ways a maternal figure as well. So that when Vanessa's love affair with Roger began, in 1911, that altered relationship put Roger in a new perspective for Virginia. With Leslie Stephen now dead for seven years, Virginia suddenly found in Roger someone to whom she could logically offer her filial devotion. Little did she dream, however, in calling Fry back to life and to utterance in her biography that he would also become a kind of secret lover to her – 'I'm so in love with him,' she wrote to Vanessa – but one whom she had created in the safe, distant shades of posthumous existence.

Leonard's description of Virginia during the height of her breakdown of 1913–15 provides us with the slightest hint of this curious attachment. In recounting the difficulties he had in inducing Virginia to see a doctor, he writes that Roger had suggested seeing a Dr Henry Head. And, despite her initial protestations, Virginia 'amazed me by saying at once that she would go to Head . . .' Probably more than anything else, it was the special character of her feeling for Roger that determined her in her choice – that is, Roger's choice – of Dr Head.

On 9 September, 1913 Virginia, with an overdose of veronal, touched the sleeve of death for a second time in her life. It must have come to her as a shock of dark significance that exactly twenty-one years later to the day – 9 September, 1934 – Roger Fry's death should occur, as though fixing in spirit forever the subtle bond which held them together.

It is hard to imagine how Virginia felt about the large responsibility of Roger Fry's reincarnation. For in death he came into her full possession. Upon her alone rested the burden of striking into shape, from an emporium of fact, something steady and permanent and whole. Conflicts must have erupted when she realized that the father-image she wished to restore was decidedly discrepant from the man she now knew him to be. Fry's ineluctable figure stared at her in the privacy of her workroom, and there was little she could do. She must be true to his memory. But she must also be true to her art. The struggle over his restoration grew steadily more impairing as time went on. How could she, cluttered with boxes of 'tailors' bills, love letters and picture postcards', light up the dim passages of his most private affairs – his daily successes, his major failings and his permanent failures? She had suddenly, she realized, become too emotionally entangled with her subject, and the archival relics heaped around her grew to be as monumental as those which might have obstructed her had she been asked to write the life of Leslie Stephen. She might rewrite the words, but she could not revise the emotion.

In recognizing the paternal aspect of Roger Fry and its connection to Vanessa, Virginia found that resurrecting him would demand a formidable price. For in making her way into a past that reached back to 1909 she could not ignore the crowded obliquities of a private history that quickened to life the memory of Leslie Stephen as well.

We have only to compare some of the letters to see how similar was her intonation of sorrow at Leslie Stephen's death to that of Roger Fry's. 'The dreadful thing', she had written in 1904 when her father died, 'is that I never did enough for him all those years . . . I never helped him as I might have done.' And again: 'If one could only tell him how one cared . . .' Now, in 1934, her words for Roger Fry: 'I still find myself thinking I shall tell him something.' '. . . I have felt since his death how little one gave him – how much I wished I had told him what he meant to me.'

In some mysterious yet absolute way Virginia held in reserve for Roger Fry the very phrasing of grief she had earlier uttered for Leslie Stephen. How much must have passed through her mind as she stood at Golders Green in that autumnal month of 1934 that recalled the leafless trees of 1904 when she had stood at Golders Green for her father. And just as she had combed through the spectral letters of her father for Maitland's life of

Leslie Stephen, so too would she break the silence of Fry's letters three decades later in readiness for her commemoration of him.

It is against some such backcloth that we must interpret what she said after finishing the biography: 'What a curious relation is mine with Roger at this moment – I who have given him a kind of shape after his death. Was he like that? I feel very much in his presence at the moment; as if I were intimately connected with him: as if we together had given birth to this vision of him: a child born of us. Yet he had no power to alter it. And yet for some years it will represent him.' She could not have known, when this note was written, that her life of Fry would represent him for forty years. But her renewed sense of power – both artistic and unabashedly procreant – was, in 1940, temporary and doubtful. For she had brooded too long in the twilit margins and worked too hard to propitiate his shade. And she could not forget Leonard's 'most rational and impersonal' criticism that much of the biography was dull and over-quoted and lifeless. Always her own severest critic, Virginia must have seen this. A haze of defeat began to close in upon her even before the book's publication: 'Today . . . I sent off my page proofs, and then have read my "Roger" for the last time . . . And I'm in the doldrums; a little sunk and open to suggestion, conveyed by the memory of Leonard's coolness, enforced by John's [Lehmann] silence, that it's one of my failures.'

The phrase 'one of my failures' suggests that she had begun to think of her books as a series of failures – *The Years, Three Guineas*, and now *Roger Fry*. But what seems actually to have happened was that, as though in obedience to some unconscious edict, she had roused from his repose the ghost of her father; so that the sepulchral father, Leslie, looked over her shoulder as she tried to inscribe the life of the surrogate-father, Roger, and she was caught in an emotional web of conflicting filial loyalties. Seen in this light, the difficulties in writing the biography of Roger Fry had their provenance in unstable emotion and not in her mastery of craft. The rainbow of imagination had somehow got wedged between blocks of granite, and she found herself trapped. Whether Virginia herself was fully aware of this we have no way of knowing. But the price exacted for assuming the responsibility of so formidable a task as Roger Fry's restoration was one that she alone would ultimately have to pay.

VITA AND VIRGINIA AND VANESSA

Nigel Nicolson

MY MOTHER, Vita Sackville-West, had very little to do with Charleston or its garden, and Vanessa never asked for her advice. But she did have quite a lot to do with Monks House garden, not with great success, because she never ceased to despair about the lack of visual taste in either of the Woolves. She once commented that Leonard was attempting to reproduce Versailles in a quarter acre of Sussex.

However, I really want to discuss her relationship with the two sisters, Virginia and Vanessa. With Vanessa, of course, it was more difficult, because Vita was extraordinarily modest about her intellectual attainments and was scared of Vanessa in a way that she wasn't of Virginia. Vanessa had a ' marmorial chastity', to use Virginia's phrase, which could be very intimidating. One knew, even I as a child, who met her very seldom, that any false step could not easily be retrieved, as happened, for instance with John Rothenstein, who remarked, I think on his very first visit to Charleston, that Titian didn't know how to draw, a remark which Vanessa never forgot or forgave. There's no doubt that her almost instant judgements and frighteningly high standards could make people who were well disposed to her into people who quaked in her presence.

There was one occasion which has been quite frequently referred to in the memoirs, biographies and diaries. It was in Berlin in 1929, when both the Woolves, Duncan and Vanessa, Quentin, and my first cousin Eddie Sackville-West and my mother and father all gathered together in that just pre-Hitler city. We were there, my brother Ben and I, as children. One evening we went to see a Russian film called *Sturm über Asien* – Storm Over Asia – a propaganda film with certain spicy interludes which were not thought suitable for people under the age of twelve. The day we went to this film happened to be my twelfth birthday, and there was a dispute at the door between my mother and the custodian on whether I should be admitted, being only just of age. The answer, in pre-Nazi days, remember, was No. Now, very often, people who are recollecting an event which happened when they were, say, thirty, are not really recollecting it at all, but recollecting what they remember of that event when they were fifty. But on this occasion, I can assure you, although I was only twelve, I remember it precisely. The awful night: it was raining, there had previously been snow, slush in the gutters, it was cold, it was dark, and everybody there had conceived for each other a certain apprehension, even dislike. Vanessa did not approve of the Nicolsons. She wrote an account of this awful evening to Roger Fry in which she said, 'I see no reason at all why Virginia has introduced these people into our society.' That was very evident. Leonard refused to come a party which my father, who was then Chargé d'Affaires at the Embassy in Berlin, had arranged for him to meet leading German politicians. My mother dragged Virginia off, that very day before the film, to Sans Souci, much to the annoyance of everybody else, and we, the boys, were bored and tired. I was refused permission to enter the cinema. My mother could be very fierce about this sort of thing. We stood on the pavement arguing. Vita said, 'Well, if he can't go in, I won't go in either.' That was very like her; she always thought that she could score off people by refusing to indulge in something that somebody else was forbidden to indulge in.

It was therefore an awkward relationship between Vanessa and Vita. Vita very seldom went to Charleston; on only two occasions that I can remember. I know I never went there at all until after Duncan's death. They met again in Rome in 1935, six years after the Berlin disaster. Vanessa wrote to Boris Anrep after this Rome visit: 'Harold isn't a bad creature, but my impression is that he could be led or pushed in any direction. Vita is as masterful as Mussolini, and has him under complete control.' How wrong people can get other people! My father was not at all pliable at that time. He was at the height of his professional competence, he'd just been elected to Parliament, he was a leading opponent of the appeasement policy. He was almost formidable, not at all the wincing creature that Vanessa suggested.

As for Vita's being Mussolini, she did have a certain imperious quality, I must admit. I remember her once at Sissinghurst, at about that time, seeing the stag hounds streaming across our fields. The stag leapt into the lake pursued by the hounds, swimming, and by the huntsman, who had taken our rowing boat which was tethered to the bank, and Vita, seeing this, seized her rifle, strode down to the lake and fired not at the stag, not at the hounds, not at the huntsman, but at our own rowing boat and sank it. Then she shouldered her still smoking rifle, while my father looked on amazed.

That, if you like, was the Mussolini side of her. But there was another, very gentle, reticent side. At the end of the War, when my brother Ben and I had returned from three years abroad in the Army in Africa and Italy, we said to her, 'Let's give a party.' We'd never given a party at Sissinghurst before, and she said, 'Good heavens, why?'

'Well, we won the war and now we're back safe and sound.'

Then she said, 'What sort of a party?' 'A cocktail party.' 'But we don't know how to make cocktails.'

Ben said, 'Well, people have written whole books on the subject, and we can find out.' And then my mother said, putting every obstacle in the way of this outlandish proposal, 'But we don't know anybody to ask', which was almost true, because, although we had many London friends, we had carefully avoided getting to know any of our neighbours.

We said, 'we know three people.' We would ask them to bring their friends; so she had to agree. Everybody who was invited naturally accepted, because they wanted to see what went on in this curious place. The party took place in the Long Library. It was terrible: we couldn't introduce anybody to anybody else, because we didn't know who they were. The cocktails were undrinkable. And at the beginning of the party a lady came up to my mother and said, 'I wonder if you can tell me who that lady in blue over there is?' 'Oh, yes,' said Vita, delighted to recognize one of the three women whom she did know, 'that's Mrs Hamilton Price.' 'No,' said the lady, 'I'm Mrs Hamilton Price.' The party never really recovered from that, and in her lifetime we never held another.

But to return to her relationship with Vanessa. They came closest on two occasions. One was when Julian Bell was killed in Spain, and Vita wrote a letter of condolence to Vanessa. Vanessa replied in a much more intimate and warmer way than she'd ever used to Vita before. She said, 'These past few weeks have been really terrible, as you can imagine. But I don't think I could have survived them without Virginia's constant presence and help. But I can't tell Virginia that. Will you tell her?' What a flood of light that throws upon the relationship of the two sisters. So close were they and yet so far apart that one couldn't express to the other her profoundest feeling of gratitude. That Vanessa should choose Vita as the intermediary was very striking, because she hardly knew her. But she knew that Vita meant to Virginia probably more than any other person in her lifetime outside her own family.

The second occasion, of course, was when Virginia herself died. A correspondence, quite brief, an exchange of about three or four letters on each side, ensued after her suicide. Vanessa asked Vita to come to Charleston. I think it was only about the second time she'd ever been there. We know very little about what transpired between them on that occasion, but it was obviously for both of them a highly emotional moment in which both were as guarded as their natures dictated, but felt that they were creating between them a bond which could never be severed. Those letters have been little quoted. I wrote a short article for the *Charleston Newsletter* about them some years ago, and I think that Frances Spalding used one or two. But in their entirety they are so moving that I think that one day they ought to be published, and I offer them now to any future biographer who cares to make use of them.

That was really the end of the relationship between Vanessa and Vita. Vita's relationship with Virginia was totally different, much closer, much warmer, and they were lovers, for about three years, between 1925 and 1928. It still seems to me to be one of the strangest affairs that we know about. Virginia had always been rather frigid in her physical relationships. She had had, as far as we know, no lesbian affair with anybody before. I can't really count that with Violet Dickinson. It led to nothing so traumatic as it did with Vita. And Virginia's relationship with Ethel Smyth had nothing of that character in it. And yet she took to this three-year relationship with Vita very calmly, without any sense of shock, or certainly not of shame, and without any fear of the consequence; but Vita had that fear. She sensed very strongly that she might trigger off in Virginia some fantasy, perhaps, which would lead to a new attack of madness. It never in fact came to anything like that, but this was constantly in my mother's mind. And so they formed this relationship based, on Vita's side, on immense admiration for Virginia as a person and as a writer. She recognized her genius, of course. She had no envy for it. She was a woman without envy. And, more humanly, as she once wrote to my father about Virginia, 'She has a sweet and childlike nature from which her intellect was completely separated.' But, she went on, of course nobody would believe this except perhaps Vanessa and Leonard.

I recognize so well that childlike nature in Virginia Woolf which was manifest even to me as a child. She was wonderful with children. It was only after you were seventeen or eighteen that she could become formidable. I well recollect times when she visited us at Long Barn, our earlier house, when she would say to my mother, 'Go away, Vita, can't you see that I'm talking to Ben and Nigel?' Now what could be more flattering to children of ten, eleven, twelve years old? We recognized that she was the leading novelist of her day. The word genius was used of her in her own lifetime. That she should want to devote hours of her time to exploring the empty minds of two little boys was something that I shall never forget. It wasn't wholly altruistic. What she was gathering was copy. As she once said to me, 'What's it like to be a child?' I said to her, 'Virginia, you know what it's like, because you've been a child. But I don't know what it's like to be grown up, because I've never been grown up.' She replied that it was something that everybody had experienced but nobody could recapture. And so she made me go through the whole of my day: 'What woke you up?', 'How did you dress?', 'Which sock, did you put on? Left or right?', 'What did you have for breakfast?' Every detail, until I walked into the room and found her there. This was, of course, her method not only with children but with adults too; she longed to explore the detail and the intimacy of their lives. Once she said to me, 'Nothing has really happened until its been described.' She meant described in writing. She meant that one must keep a diary. She said:

You must write letters, to your mother and father and

> brother, and they must keep them, and you keep theirs. The whole of your life, which you will never be able to recover later, must be put into writing. When you write you must imagine yourself knocking up in the squash court by yourself, trying out strokes, verbal strokes, without fear that other people are looking on to mock you. You must write, write and write.

Not very much of Bloomsbury intruded upon our lives as children. My mother called it Gloomsbury. She transmitted to us some of her own fear of these clever people. It was rather scarifying. The one person who rescued us from that was Clive Bell. I recall one occasion at Long Barn. I must have been eight, I think, and there was a large party and a lot of the Bloomsbury people were there at luncheon, and they made thirteen. For some reason people in those days minded sitting down thirteen at table, and I was brought down to make the fourteenth, beside my mother at the end of the table. Opposite to me there was an extraordinary woman, like a parakeet, with a very made-up face, a great beak nose and a huge hat. It was of course Ottoline Morrell. Suddenly there was a pause in the general conversation, and into that silence I dropped the words, 'Mummy, is that lady a witch?' Everybody heard it. Even Bloomsbury was a little taken aback. Then Clive said from the other end of the table: 'Of course she is, of course she is, and we've all longed to say so. And you, Nigel, have now told the truth.' That saved the situation. He was very much like that.

But perhaps the most lasting memory I have of that group is when Virginia was writing *Orlando*. We didn't know – naturally, in 1928 I was eleven years old – the precise relationship between Vita and Virginia. A woman who was a friend of both of them, who should have known much better, said to me once at that time, 'I suppose you realize that Virginia loves your mother?' I replied, with the innocence of eleven years old, 'Well, of course she does, we all do.' That was how, slowly and gradually, the realization of their relationship dawned upon us.

Virginia took us to Knole – I have a photograph of the occasion – and she took us through the rooms, and looked at all the portraits on the walls and asked us who they all were, these long dead Sackvilles. Of course we didn't really know, but we and she made up stories about them. Then we came back, and the book was published. Even Vita had not read a single word of it or knew any more than that she was the subject of it until she received a copy of it, and the manuscript fully bound, on publication day. Then we read it too. I remember that my only reaction was one of distress, because at the very end of the book, as you may remember, Orlando has a child, a son. And we protested: 'But, Virginia, there are two of us. Where's the other?'

Those are a few recollections of my mother in this company to which she didn't really belong. She was accepted as Virginia's friend. She never became, except for the two occasions that I've mentioned, intimate with Vanessa. She was frightened of Leonard Woolf, whom she thought, quite wrongly, grim. But with Virginia she established and maintained a relationship even long after their love affair had ended which was beautiful in its simplicity and the genuine pleasure they took in each other's company. The honesty of it – Virginia's honesty about Vita's writing, which she could convey without offence. And Vita's love for her which was sustained after many, many years. When Vita had fallen in love with other people Virginia remained the person who was central to her life, apart from my father. You can still see her photograph upon her desk at Sissinghurst.

VIRGINIA AND ROSE

Jane Emery

'POTTERISM . . . by Rose Macaulay, a don's book, hard-headed, masculine, atmosphere of lecture rooms, not interesting to me . . .'
The Diary of Virginia Woolf, Vol. II Tuesday, 10 August, 1920.
'Poor dear Rose, judging from her works, is a Eunuch – that's what I dislike about *Potterism*: she has no parts.'
The Letters of Virginia Woolf, Vol. VI Letter to Hope Mirrlees, end October 1920.

As a diarist Virginia Woolf writes of others both hyperbolically and harshly, sometimes in the same sentence. But she writes in the imagined presence of a wise and distanced judge – the diary's future reader: 'Old Virginia, putting on her spectacles'. The contradictions in the portraits are lifelike; the likenesses are meant to endure. ('The lady of 50 will be able to say how near to the truth I come.') Her letters, however, were written with a different purpose and to a different audience. Her correspondent was for the moment her dearest friend, who was to be persuaded by amusing caricatures to adore Virginia and none other.

Both Virginias can be heard in the title comments about Rose Macaulay's seventh novel and first international best-seller, written before the two had met. Neither her rejection of *Potterism*'s authorial voice nor the *ad feminam* attack on Rose herself prophesies a friendship. Yet, between the first strained appearance of Rose Macaulay as a dinner guest of the Woolfs in Richmond in 1921 and Virginia Woolf's death twenty years later, despite some barriers between their literary worlds, a genial relationship developed; its slow growth played a part in each life. We can reconstruct its progress, even though the Blitz destroyed Virginia Woolf's letters to Rose Macaulay and there never was a Rose

Macaulay diary.

Here is material for a novelist rather than for a critic – a chapter about two writers' differing temperaments, *milieux*, reputations and middle-age changes. 'Virginia and Rose' can be read as one of the many minor subplots of their lives. Because both writers had a gift for social comedy, the tone should not be grave. Each looked at the other to define herself; the ironies of their mutual scrutiny are amusing.

Who was Rose Macaulay in 1921 and why did the Woolfs invite her to dine? Ever insatiably curious, Virginia Woolf decided to 'enlarge her sphere' by entertaining people who were outside Bloomsbury and Mayfair. She may well have been introduced to Rose Macaulay at the 1917 Club, where both the Woolfs and Rose Macaulay often lunched or took tea. Despite her negative pre-judgement, Virginia Woolf discovered that to know Rose Macaulay was neither to risk boredom nor to venture very far from her own background. Both were descendants of what Noël Annan has called 'the intellectual aristocracy'; both were daughters in the large family of an agnostic Cambridge don. And both had gone swimming with Rupert Brooke. Rose had read Modern History at Somerville College and was as rigorous about language as any Apostle. 'After all', Virginia Woolf was to write in her 1926 diary, 'she has no humbug about her; is exactly on a par as conventions go, I imagine.' Virginia also had, as Leonard Woolf wrote, 'a streak of the common-sense, down to earth, granitic quality of mind and soul characteristic in many generations of her father's family'.

As a dinner guest in demand in literary London, Rose Macaulay was known for her comic use of reason to expose sham. She scintillated as a jester – an entertainer with a nimble and irreverent wit. By 1921, at forty (one year older than Virginia), she had found her social and literary style; her attractions were her intelligence and her *élan vital*. Her movements, thought and speech were quick. Storm Jameson described her as 'enchanting to watch, a narrow head with small curls, like a Greek head in a museum, with that way she had of speaking in arpeggios'. And she was more complex than Virginia guessed. Although more than one witness described her tall, thin figure as sexless, the 'Eunuch' was losing her struggle against her love for a married man at the very time she was setting forth in *Potterism* the hero's hard-headed argument against the exaltation of sexual love.

Rose Macaulay had found a bookish, upper middle-class public for her topical, lightly satirical novels of ideas. *Potterism*'s target was the corrupt power of the post-War popular press; although the story was told from four points of view, its form was conventional. Rose was never interested in aesthetic theories; in fact, although her literary and historical knowledge was formidable, she knew little about painting and thought discussion of the art of The Novel tedious. Her amusing novels were ingenious variations of traditional genres. In contrast, Virginia Woolf was beginning, as she exulted, to find a new form for the novel, a 'shape' to enclose 'this, loose, drifting material of life'. Up to this point her work had achieved a *succès d'estime*, but for some time it was to remain caviare to the general. Leonard later wrote of the reception of *Jacob's Room* in 1923 that he was publishing a book which the vast majority of people, including booksellers and the 'literary establishment', condemned as unintelligible or absurd. But in 1923 *Potterism* went into its eleventh printing.

At no time, however, could Rose Macaulay's novels fit Leonard Woolf's damning description of most contemporary best-sellers: 'written by second-class writers whose psychological brew contains a touch of sentimentality, the story-telling gift, and a mysterious sympathy with the daydreams of ordinary people'. Her books had their own value as intelligent comedy and social criticism, but she was always to be modest about them and was an early admirer of Virginia Woolf. The woman of talent recognized the woman of genius.

Not surprisingly, Rose was self-conscious when she came to dine with the Woolfs. As her character Daisy Simpson, a popular novelist, thinks in *Keeping Up Appearances*, you could not be yourself quite with anyone who matters to you. As late as 1926 Virginia spoke slightingly of Rose's manner as a guest, calling her 'chittery-chattery'. She added: 'But this was partly nerves, I think; she felt us alien and observant, doubtless.'

Virginia Woolf's account of their first shared evening is mixed.

> Rose Macaulay dined here last week – something like a lean sheep-dog in appearance – harum scarum – humble – too much of a professional, yet just on the intellectual side of the border. Might be religious, though; mystical perhaps. I daresay she observes more than one thinks for. Clear, pale mystical eyes. A kind of faded beauty; oh badly dressed. I don't suppose we shall ever meet for she lives with Royde-Smith & somehow won't come to grips with us.

Rose's housemate was Naomi Royde-Smith, literary editor of the *Westminster Gazette*: she fancied herself as a bluestocking. Woolf attended one of Rose and Naomi's Thursday evenings and was horrified at what she saw as the complacent respectability of the middling guests, although on other occasions such literary lights as W.B. Yeats, Edith Sitwell and Aldous Huxley attended. Even more repulsive was a 'ghastly' dinner party which Rose gave in a restaurant in 1926. (Rose refused all domestic responsibility.) Virginia and Leonard arrived late from the press, still in their working clothes. Virginia described the other guests as '10 second rate writers in second rate dress clothes . . . I won't in any spasm of hypocritical humanity include Wolves'. Virginia excluded herself and Leonard on the ground that this company was 'a thin-blooded set; so "nice", "kind", respectable, cleverish & in the swim'. And she thanked God she was out of journalism, 'no longer brother in arms with Rose & Robert and Sylvia [Lynd]'.

Virginia Woolf is here distinguishing between her world and Rose's – between 'intellectual' and 'professional'. Although Virginia's earnings from 1919 to 1924 came chiefly from literary journalism, she despised the commercial competitiveness of what she called 'the underworld'. Like Virginia, Rose prized 'the intellectual side' – what she called the culture of 'the fastidious and the fine in mind'. She hoped to increase her income enough to give up writing newspaper feature stories. (She asked herself, as did her character Daisy, 'Why would they not let her write about inhuman things, about books, about religions, about places, about the world at large, about things of which intelligent persons have heard?')

After Rose and Naomi parted, however, Rose often dined

with the Woolfs. Leonard liked her, Vita and Harold liked her, T.S. Eliot and Morgan Forster liked her. Vita had met her when both worked for the War Office in 1917; thirty-three years later Rose was a much-enjoyed house guest for the Christmas holidays at Sissinghurst. By the Fifties Forster had become one of Rose's best friends. To her surprise perhaps, this outsider was welcomed in Bloomsbury and Virginia always candidly admitted to jealousy. Elizabeth Bowen believed that Virginia Woolf's law for her friends was 'Thou shalt have none other God but me.' And she was further vexed that Rose Macaulay thought E.M. Forster the finest novelist in England.

Observing Rose's compatibility with this select company, Virginia sometimes recorded an approving shock of recognition; one diary entry reads, 'In some lights she has the beautiful eyes of all us distinguished women writers: the refinement, the clearness of cut; the patience; & humbleness.' But through the Twenties and even early Thirties Virginia wrote of her dismay at the damage she believed had been wrought upon Rose Macaulay's mind and character by being a freelance writer and public figure. As a university educated historian Rose was an entertaining social critic, but Virginia disapproved of her lunching at the League of Nations, speaking at dinners and giving opinions to newspapers. 'As a successful lady novelist she has become rather jealous, spiteful and uneasy about Bloomsbury; can talk of nothing but reviews.' 'I think . . . that she is jealous, & test whatever else she says with a view to finding out whether she is or not . . . but I may imagine it: & it shows my own jealousy no doubt as suspicions always do.' (But Harold Nicolson described Rose Macaulay's spirit as that of 'splendid charity'.)

Only occasionally Woolf acknowledged her own rare freedom as an author-publisher in contrast to Rose: 'I'm the only woman in England free to write what I like.' And in 1934 she acknowledged the protection which her marriage gave to her as an artist by saying of Rose: 'She is a ravaged sensitive old hack – as I should be, no doubt, save for L.'

Realizing her privileges also made her realize her ambivalence about her comparative isolation from the popular forum. When assessing her own career against that of 'our leading lady novelists', she admitted in the diary 'I am not quite one of them. I saw my own position a good deal lowered & diminished; & this is part of the value of seeing new people.' But, on the defensive, she continually compared herself to Rose, using her as a scapegoat. She found Rose's faults similar to, but worse than, what she saw as her own: 'I am not so nice as I was, but I am nicer than Rose Macaulay.' She criticized Rose's dress, yet she was self-conscious about her own. She scorned her for sensitivity about reviews, yet she suffered from the same skinless vulnerability. She wrote in a state of deep concentration, yet of Rose she said, 'How she grinds!' She withdrew from her sexual life, yet she calls Rose 'a spindle-shanked withered virgin'.

And she ridiculed 'Old Rose' in her letters. To Quentin Bell she described her as 'a mummified cat'. But if Rose sensed this mockery, she did not suffer. She seems to have been aware of the unattractive pictures Virginia drew of other people and she understood the compulsions of her wickedly playful imagination. In one of the eulogies she wrote after Virginia's death, Rose said, 'For it amused her to embellish, fantasticate and ironize her friends, as she embellished, fantasticated and ironized all she wrote of.' And to her friend Father Johnson she wrote: 'She had so much fun, and humour, and a kind of genial friendliness, though also much malicious comment (discreetly *not* published).'

Rose Macaulay was helped, not harmed, by their relationship. She too, as Victor Gollancz testified, was a snob; she was bored by 'tedious and uninteresting members of the middle class'. She implicitly expressed her desire to be welcomed in Bloomsbury's world in *Keeping Up Appearances*, a comedy of the split personality of the popular novelist-journalist (much less distinguished than Rose herself) who longs to mix with people of high culture.

The Hogarth Press supported her aspirations to accept fewer journalistic assignments. In 1926 Virginia and Leonard Woolf published *Catchwords and Claptrap*, Rose's monograph attacking jargon and cant, and in 1931 they published *Some Religious Elements in English Literature*. Continuing the research which led to that critical study, Macaulay followed it with her historical novel about the Civil War, *They Were Defeated* (Collins, 1932). Although fresh and original, it may well owe some of its inspiration to Woolf's story of Shakespeare's sister in *A Room of One's Own* (1929), for it is in part the story of a young girl who strives to be a poet and is destroyed by the male world.

Having happily begun a period of intense research, Rose

Macaulay published a controversial biography of Milton with Duckworth (1934). And in 1938, aided by an inheritance which gave her independence, she published *The Writings of E.M. Forster* with Hogarth. She did not stop writing her astringent comedies, but she now had more than one audience.

With this strengthening of their intellectual relationship, an increasingly warm friendship developed. Through the late Thirties both writers, more secure, began to discover mutual sympathies and interests. Virginia's diary begins to mention Rose with mild but familiar affection, and from the late Thirties her name appears in the Woolf social schedule. Virginia always said no writer could swallow a contemporary, but she read Rose's Spanish Civil War novel *And No Man's Wit* (1940) – perhaps because of Julian Bell. She may even have had the form of Rose Macaulay's *Told By An Idiot* (1923) in her imagination when she began the early version of *The Years* as an 'essay-novel'. In 1940 she writes of her admiration for Rose's ambulance-driving during the Blitz. And she mentions Rose, 'to whom I mean to write', and notes having talked to her from 4 to 6.30. Virginia discovered that the rational Rose, who wrote an enchanted review of *Orlando*, was, like herself, a comic fantasist, and that both were drawn to the subject of androgyny. Virginia's feminist position grew stronger, both were increasingly indignant about the disadvantages of being a woman. When war threatened, both opposed it. Virginia may have arrived at more understanding of Rose's life as an independent writer. The affectionate but undemonstrative Rose discovered that Virginia not only craved but required demonstrations of affection. On 10 October, 1940 she wrote her:

> How I wish I could see you! It's one of the sad things about this war, seeing people has become so much more difficult, at the same time more important . . . I would like to talk about Coleridge some time, as I have long had in mind a novel about a girl who would be his descendant (great great grandchild, the fruit of mild and rural sin) and would take after him.

Soon after Virginia invited her for a weekend at Rodmell. But the war continued to keep them apart.

The story of the growing mutual sympathy between these

two writers ends abruptly with the horror of Virginia Woolf's suicide. Although Rose Macaulay wrote two eloquent public tributes to her, the most moving expression of the loss she felt after twenty years of knowing Virginia Woolf was private. To Leonard she wrote: 'She is the one person, who *should* not have died, who cannot be spared. No one like her could ever be.'

This article is a revision of material in Chapter II of *Rose Macaulay: A Writer's Life* by Jane Emery, John Murray, 1991.

ETHEL CAME TO LUNCH

Quentin Bell

VIRGINIA WOOLF died in 1941 and to many people it then seemed that her reputation would die with her. The men and women who make opinions in universities, in the media, in editorial offices and upon other seats of judgement, condemned her. She was a snob, a *rentier*, she told malicious stories about her friends, she lived in Bloomsbury. It followed – for the moral purity of our censors is exquisite, their judgements rigorous – that Virginia Woolf was without talent and had better be forgotten. In the Fifties and Sixties it seemed that this advice had been heeded: like Bloomsbury itself, Mrs Woolf was dismissed. True, her publisher took a different view: he pointed out that her novels continued to sell very nicely thank you. But Leonard Woolf was clearly biassed. Another voice, that of Desmond MacCarthy, was also raised, but so far as I know only in private. About a year after Virginia's death he prophesied that her reputation would slump. 'But,' he added, 'there is a cyclical movement, and it will rise again.' He did not live to see how good a prophet he had been.

In the late Sixties I was engaged in writing Virginia's life. 'A pity', they said, 'that no one will be interested.' But presently it seemed that some people *were* interested; and then it appeared that America, God bless her, was very much interested. This transatlantic rumour grew into a mighty roar which, crossing the oceans, has been picked up in this country and disseminated through the world. When therefore *The New Yorker* in March of this year announced a revival of the kind of hostility towards Virginia and Bloomsbury with which I was so familiar years ago, I suspected that Desmond's cycle was still turning. The same article also recorded that some sharp criticisms were coming from what might seem an unexpected source – the feminists. I found this interesting in that I had myself suggested that Virginia Woolf's feminism (she detested the word, but I can find no other) was not entirely suited to a modern feminist audience. Such an audience might rejoice in the argumentative power of *A Room of One's Own*, but the tone was too mild, too conciliatory. Virginia believed in tolerance, she believed in persuasion; in a word, she was unheroic. In 1938 she could say with proud assurance: 'scarcely a human being in the course of history has fallen to a woman's rifle'. Today that statement seems less unquestionably true, for today women in the United States and elsewhere have been armed and trained as soldiers. To what extent that development has been welcomed by American feminists I do not know, but certainly it would have been deplored by the author of *A Room of One's Own*. All of which leads me to wonder whether our transatlantic cousins might not now prefer a Suffragette to a Suffragist.

These terms require some words of explanation. The National Union of Women's Suffrage Societies, formed in 1897 under the leadership of Mrs Fawcett and usually referred to as the 'Suffragists', worked for the same reforms as the Women's Social and Political Union – the 'Suffragettes' – created in 1907 and dominated by Mrs Pankhurst and her daughter Christabel. The Suffragists believed in the value of rational argument and were averse to violence of any kind. The Suffragettes were not. Naturally it was the Suffragettes who captured the attention of the public and who are remembered today. It was not simply that they marched to the sound of splintering glass and outraged feelings; they displayed military virtues of the highest order: superb tactical invention, good staff work, prudent audacity, heroic stoicism and unshakeable discipline; they excelled in all these things. And when, in 1914, their battle still unwon, they turned from civil to international strife, it was a thousand pities that the Pankhursts were not given command of the Allied armies and had to content themselves with urging their countrymen towards the killing grounds commanded by their inept brothers.

When the War was over, Mrs Pankhurst and Christabel found their occupation gone: Englishwomen over the age of thirty had been given the vote, a gift which somehow did not seem quite so precious as it had appeared while it was still being fought for. And when, three years later, complete equality was achieved (without fuss or violence of any kind), Mrs Pankhurst had but a month to live and the Suffragettes were ancient history. But the struggle was by no means over, for a suffragist appeared to carry on the battle in her own way. In October 1928 Virginia Woolf gave two lectures to the women's colleges at Cambridge. These were rewritten and published a year later as *A Room of One's Own*. There must have been many veterans from the heroic past who read those persuasive arguments and devastating ironies with the delighted feeling that they had gained an ally. And there was one notable suffragette who, reading the book, fell in love with its author and hurried round to 52 Tavistock Square. She was Ethel Smyth.

> An old woman of seventy-one has fallen in love with me. It is at once hideous and horrid and melancholy sad. It is like being caught by a giant crab.

Thus Virginia, writing to me in May 1930. I was living abroad and at that time had to take my aunt's complaints on trust, but even then I did not believe that Dame Ethel was so hideous and horrid as Virginia suggested. Nor was she. She had been a militant, having given two years for the cause; she had broken windows, been thrown into prison, and for a time had been very much in love with Mrs Pankhurst. She was indeed one of nature's suffragettes, tremendously brave and tremendously vigorous, riding very straight to hounds and demanding vociferously that her rights as a musician should be recognized, mocking, scolding, complaining. She was, like Mrs Pankhurst, a staunch conservative and, unlike that lady, the daughter of a general, the companion of an empress and a friend of Kaiser Wilhelm II.

I cannot remember in what circumstances I met her. It was at Charleston and I think that she arrived by accident, for otherwise I do not see why I should have carried her bags across the fields down to the Swingates where she could catch a bus. At any rate she was gracious and grateful for my services. I liked her and longed to ask her to sit for her portrait. I hadn't the courage, and in truth a Rembrandt was needed to deal properly with Ethel as an old woman. That immensely strong face, surmounted by a wild disorder of hair, above which was an even more wildly improbable hat, was, as one may say, almost too paintable to be painted.

What she thought of me I am not sure. Virginia, always a mistress of romantic fiction, reported that 'she adores you . . . and would marry you, given a dog's chance'. Also she said that

I was like a dog. True, she qualified this by saying 'a sheep-dog'. That was not quite the impression that I, as a young man, was trying to create. But it is *her* character that concerns me, and it must be said that one could not but admire her courage and her fortitude, her panache and her fun. Of her music I cannot speak, but certainly there is something tremendously engaging about her writing; she may sometimes be absurd, she is often very amusing, and she is always highly readable. Why then did Virginia say that it was like being caught by a giant crab? Well, I think that this *was* what it was like. Virginia enjoyed Ethel's good qualities very much, but she did want to call her soul her own, and if you are attached to a giant crab, a crab which pinches and will not let go, a crab which demands love, makes scenes and is perpetually bombarding you with questions and assertions, you begin to feel that your soul is being taken over. And yet it was Ethel who felt that she was the aggrieved party. She was much more in love with Virginia than Virginia was with her, and she suffered. They parted company and then, because Virginia did indeed like her, they were reconciled – until the next quarrel.

I did not see much of this painful business, but I remember one meeting which gave me a taste of it. It began at an exhibition at Agnew's, where I ran into the Woolfs with Ethel. Ethel was complaining loudly of the manner in which she had been treated by I know not what conductor. It was a long and involved tale, and clearly Leonard and Virginia had heard it already. I had really come to look at pictures, but Leonard persuaded me to accompany them home in a taxi, and it was in the taxi that Leonard, trusting to poor Ethel's deafness, said to me: 'Can't you shut her up, Quentin?' Unfortunately he had not realized that the interior of a taxi may serve as a kind of sounding box in which even the deaf may hear. Ethel heard; and the situation which had been tedious became unpleasant. By the time we got to Tavistock Square, Ethel had changed her tack. Seeking, I fear, to annoy Leonard, she had begun to abuse the Socialists. She was very rude about them, and I, foolishly no doubt, produced arguments to which she hardly listened and could perhaps hardly hear, but I fear that she heard enough to demote me from the status of sheep dog to that of mongrel.

Bernard Shaw had recently published a book called *The*

Intelligent Woman's Guide to Socialism, and this excited her scorn and anger. Virginia, who was thoroughly bored by all this, tried to change the subject, but in vain. She went on and on with really dreadful persistence until at last Leonard could no longer resist the obvious retort 'Perhaps it was not addressed to you, Ethel.'

Stopped in mid-career, she asked Leonard what he had said. He had to repeat himself twice, speaking very loudly, before the remark could be understood.

When later I heard that Ethel was coming to Charleston, I was a little worried at the prospect of meeting her again. It was foolish of me. If she remembered my perversity, it was most certainly forgiven; it was probably forgotten.

But I must explain why Ethel was at Charleston. In truth, she had now fallen in love with Vanessa. It was a little inconsistent of her to do so, for Ethel detested Bloomsbury. She had made an exception when she fell in love with Virginia, and a further more dubious exception in the case of Leonard; but to proceed from that and conceive a passion for Virginia's sister was surely carrying inconsistency rather far. Nor was that all: she was extremely friendly with Duncan Grant. She was one of that fairly large class of people who detested Bloomsbury but did not carry their enmity to the point of disliking the company of those members of the group whom they happened to meet. Nor can it be said that those whom Ethel liked made any enormous effort to please her. Vanessa, with her sister's example before her and being of a more cautious temperament – also, it should be said, being quite indifferent to the rights and wrongs of her sex – was in no hurry to respond to Ethel's advances. 'You are a little like your sainted sister,' observed Ethel.

Nevertheless there she was at Charleston, having lunch with Vanessa, Duncan, my sister and myself. She had at some time written the score of a ballet entitled *Fête Galante*. I do not know whether the music had received public performance, but the ballet had not been staged. Now I think someone influential had seen that the composition had merits. Also, Ethel had a hoard, a sum of money called 'Last Illness Fund'. She decided that she would rather have a ballet than a last illness and was ready to spend the fund – a typically spirited decision. Scenery and costumes would need to be designed, and this was where Vanessa came in. So here was Ethel come to lunch to tell us all about it. If I remember rightly, Ethel began on another topic, a new novel by Maurice Baring. She told us at some length about the plot and explained why in her opinion the book was a masterpiece. Fortunately, Virginia being absent, there was no one to contradict her. The painters were quite ready to take Maurice Baring on trust. Then, towards the end of the meal, she turned to the matter in hand. She described, and went on describing, the plot of *Fête Galante*, and then, noticing that she was sitting with her back to a piano, she turned and began to illustrate her meaning with her music. It was an extraordinary, a stupendous, performance that I remember very clearly. What I had forgotten until my sister reminded me was the deplorable fact that she and I disgraced ourselves. I must try, although it will not be easy, to mitigate our offence. Ethel, it must be explained, was in full fig. Despite the fact that it was a warm summer's day, she was lunching in a tremendously tailored tweed suit, she was crowned with one of her astonishing tricornes, she was attacking the piano as though it had been a music critic, and the piano was obviously getting the worst of it; she sang out in what seemed to us an odd manner in harmony with the music, only breaking off to exclaim in a voice as powerful as that of a huntsman who sees the fox breaking covert: 'A simple melody, a simple melody, as simple as Beethoven!' It was this, I think, which led me to exchange glances with Angelica – not, I hope, actually to giggle, but rather to lose that proper stance in which a member of the home team should listen to the music of a guest. Unfortunately we were observed, and felt in disgrace – not that Ethel stopped for a moment.

But she seemed still in a sunny mood when, after lunch, we went out into the walled garden in the hope that there might be a cooling breeze. Breeze or no breeze, Ethel went on talking, and talking, and talking . . . She was talking, I think, about herself, and she talked principally to Vanessa. Presently we found ourselves at that north-eastern corner of the walled garden which now bears some mosaics and a pool. At this point we, the disgraceful young, had fallen to the rear. Ethel was walking, talking with Vanessa and Duncan; they turned up the path that leads back towards the house and after a step or two Duncan fell back and joined us. 'I think I am going to faint,' he said. 'I'm too bored to stand any more.' We found a seat for him, leaving Vanessa to carry on the battle alone. I like to think that I went to her assistance, but I am afraid that it is improbable. Also, it would be nice to be able to say that *Fête Galante* was in every way an enormous success; in fact I do not think it ever got danced.

Nobody comes badly out of this story, except of course my sister and myself, and Angelica was little more than a child. Vanessa and Duncan were indeed victims, but not the victims of any ill-will. Ethel clearly had no notion of the pain she was inflicting on them – or on Virginia, for that matter; she simply felt the need to testify, to proclaim the excellence of her art, the rightness of her opinions, her immense and unswerving faith in herself. To do that she had only to pour out her soul, and she had so much soul to pour out that poor Duncan, the weaker vessel, could not contain the awful weight of testimony.

Had Ethel been a Suffragist, she might have been more careful of feelings, approaching her listeners upon common ground, seasoning her arguments with wit, sugaring the pill of faith with a tactful placebo. But Ethel was a Suffragette: she disdained such artifices, she proclaimed the truth as she saw it, sword in hand, and was in consequence a dead bore. So perhaps was Joan of Arc. It is an occupational disease of heroes and heroines, and Ethel was certainly heroic; which is why, in a nation defended by a corps of Amazons, many may find her more to their taste than a Suffragist like Virginia.

THE LAST ARTIST

Penelope Fitzgerald

VIRGINIA WOOLF began *Between the Acts* in the spring of 1938 and finished it on 23 November 1940. The finally-arrived-at title suggests that in this last novel everything of importance will happen in the intervals. Perhaps so, but it is the pageant itself, the pageant in the gardens of Poyntz Hall, with cows in the next field, swallows overhead and a donkey engine somewhere in the bushes, which creates 'the token of some real thing behind appearances'.

Readers often find the action of the book stranger than Virginia Woolf intended. Pageants were as much part of country life between the World Wars as jumble sales (which have survived). They were popular (or assumed to be popular) fund-raisers, involving all those of goodwill. E.M. Forster, for example, wrote two pageants, one for the parish of Abinger, another, *England's Pleasant Land*, for the Surrey District Preservation Society. T. S. Eliot's *The Rock* was written for the London diocesan church-building fund. Up in Radnorshire, in the Thirties, I saw a pageant in which the ghost of the Black Vaughan was played, in fact, by the secretary of the local bowls club, who could be relied upon to aim straight, and this illustrates the curious interplay in a local pageant of fantasy and reality. Hitches, disasters and bizarre incidents were expected.

To all this, Virginia Woolf, who in 1940 was elected treasurer of the Rodmell Women's Institute, has remained true in *Between the Acts*. The pageant at Poyntz Hall is in aid of the church lighting, and actually raises thirty-six pounds, ten shillings and eight pence. She is true, also, in a poet's sense, to the central idea which gave some dignity even to the most wretched of pageants, the idea, that is, of passing time: 'It would take till midnight unless they skipped. Early Britons; Plantaganets; Tudors; Stuarts – she ticked them off, but probably she had forgotten a reign or two.' As a general rule, the organizers skipped nothing, carried on through rain or shine, and overran until night fell. At Poyntz Hall, time is presented, not through local history, but through the changing forms of English literature which Virginia Woolf (like Joyce in the maternity hospital section of *Ulysses*) imitates in turn. And these scenes too run on, with two long intervals, into 'the tender, the fading, the uninquisitive but searching light of evening'.

The pageant's organizer is awkward, hard-drinking, lesbian Miss La Trobe, by no means popular in the village. In spite of, or because of, her oddness, she has 'a passion for getting things up' – a definition as good as any other of the artist. As an artist, however, she is strikingly different from the painter Lily Briscoe in *To the Lighthouse*. Lily's picture may, in the end, never be seen at all, and she no longer cares about this. Miss La Trobe, on the other hand, demands an instant reaction and true communication. Threatened by inattention and shallowness, knowing herself to be grotesque, she dominates her audience from her retreat in the bushes. 'Hadn't she, for twenty-five minutes, made them see?' The impending war (aircraft are passing overhead in formation) is a distraction only. Virginia Woolf did not believe – as she had written to Benedict Nicolson – that the artist is able to change the course of history. War is not Miss La Trobe's concern, and nature itself takes her part. The cows bellow, the rain falls and stops, precisely at the right time to cover a difficult moment in her production when the illusion threatens to fade. It is the rector, trying to say a few words, who is interrupted by the noise of the aircraft.

If Miss La Trobe is less afraid of life than Lily Briscoe, she is also more human than Bernard, the wordmaster of *The Waves*. 'What a sense of the tolerableness of life the lights in the bedrooms of small shopkeepers give us,' says Bernard, and we feel (as Virginia Woolf probably intended) like hitting him. But Miss La Trobe, unlike Lily, unlike Bernard, is in there struggling, 'making everyone do something', brandishing her manuscript in the face of Mrs Clark from the shop, old Mrs Otter from the end house and Albert, the village idiot, and impelling them into transformation. They call her Old Bossy, but do not disobey. This closeness of Miss La Trobe to her material corresponds to a noble, but unappeasable, longing which Virginia Woolf felt for all the later part of her writing life: 'I always sit next the conductor in an omnibus and try to get him to tell me what it is like – being a conductor. In whatever company I am I try to know what it is like – being a conductor, being a woman with ten children and thirty-five shillings a week . . .' Miss La Trobe does know, otherwise she would not be able to transform.

The unlikely harmony she creates cannot last for long. At the end of the pageant, she remains awkwardly stooped over the grass, as though looking for something, so as to avoid being thanked or misunderstood. Then, when everyone else has gone, she trudges off, carrying her heavy suitcase. She accepts that, in spite of what she has offered them, the villagers have made her an outcast. The terror of this, however, does not grow any less with time.

> From the earth green waters seemed to rise over her. She took her voyage away from the shore, and raising her hand, fumbled for the latch of the iron entrance gate.

DESMOND MacCARTHY: A MEMOIR OF AFFECTION

James MacGibbon

'I'M OF Bloomsbury but I'm not *in* it', Desmond MacCarthy once told me. The occasion, a privileged one for me (I was only nineteen), was when Putnam & Co., who employed me, were wrestling with him to collect his writings for publication in book form. Desmond was a procrastinator – when it suited him – and I don't think he was enamoured of the plan. Indeed he told me once he had 'given up' because his work fell so far short of the standards set by Leslie Stephen. However, we persevered and, somehow, six volumes were gathered together in the Thirties, and it was my job to call on him at Wellington Square in Chelsea from time to time to wrest some more essays from him. Sometimes he would be still in bed, at others he would be dictating his *Sunday Times* review, albeit on Saturday morning when the literary editor must have been well nigh frantic with anxiety over losing his lead article on the book pages. He would often have plausible excuses to offer for not being ready: he had not finished his piece on Bloomsbury for 'it was not quite right'. Indeed, it never was finished and some twenty years later Robert Kee included it in *Memories* (published after his death in 1953), sadly sub-titled 'An Unfinished Memoir'. This was the first of three posthumous books.

But the frustration was Putnam's, not mine. Indeed my gain, for Desmond was always benevolent and in this way I came to know him. I expect he was amused by a young man's persistence which never threatened, and he grew to accept me as a youth who wanted to be, so to speak, his impresario. On another occasion he was 'sorry not to have me in' because Roger Fry had died. He was visibly upset – but still courteous. When it came to the proof stage of his books he would drop in at the office in Covent Garden and listen to any trivial points I had to make, even accepting some amendments. He had become bored, I suspect, and in any case he was always happy to leave proof-reading to others. Once or twice when our sessions were over he would ask me out to lunch – the first time I had been in public with a literary giant, as I regarded him. The first time, to my utter surprise, because I had been expecting to go to the Athenaeum or perhaps the Beefsteak, he walked me into the Royal Automobile Club, his long overcoat flying behind him, with a kind of bravado that made me wonder if he belonged – he certainly never drove a car. On another occasion we 'dropped in' at the Café de Paris, a place I would never have dared to enter even if I had known they served luncheon. It was deeply flattering to be in the company of a distinguished literary figure, albeit a slightly eccentric one who insisted on keeping his overcoat by him. He kept up a continuous flow of conversation consisting, for the most part, of anecdotes about the great. How, for instance, he had been invited as a young man to big house-parties, eager to know 'lions'. At one such Saturday-to-Monday a 'great statesman' was present (I now think it may have been Asquith, whom Desmond came to know well) and he seized his opportunity when he saw the important guest enter the library one morning, to read on his own.

> Imagine my surprise when, allowing for a tactful passage of time, I opened the door to see him with tears streaming down his cheeks! Assuming he had had very bad news, I withdrew. To my astonishment, an hour or two later, he was the centre of attraction at the luncheon table, talking and joking at the top of his bent, when I heard his quiet aside to the lady on my left: 'I was reading the new Marie Corelli this morning. I confess I was rather moved'.

Desmond enjoyed the joke all over again: 'Rather *moved*!' – with the infectious chuckle that was one of the characteristics that made him the liveliest of raconteurs – and broadcasters. (He was brilliant on the BBC, where he felt – and was – at his most convivial.)

Then the luncheon parties at Garrick's Villa, his last home. Molly, his wife, was acutely deaf and Desmond sat next to her. She had in her day published two delightful books, a novel and a memoir of Eton when her father was Vice-Provost. When one of the guests suggested that she should write another book

Desmond roared into her ear, 'Yes, Molly, *do*! I have always wanted to be *Mister* Henry Wood.' He always, seemed to enjoy his conversation as much as his listeners – perhaps the key to his art.

It is not for me to praise his work as a critic. Raymond Mortimer, Cyril Connolly and David Cecil have done that in their forewords to his posthumous books. I do know, though, that he delighted in praising work whenever he could: 'I wanted to give that young writer a present,' he once remarked. And when he praised his enthusiasm was infectious. To my certain knowledge Rex Warner's *Men and Gods* and Noël Annan's *Leslie Stephen* benefited hugely from his reviews – the latter in two parts on successive Sundays. He also did long stints as drama critic, and perhaps his greatest love was for the theatre. I remember his telling me, 'It is no good being a theatre critic unless, every time the lights go down, you get *terrifically* excited.' It was his enduring, youthful enthusiasm that made him so influential. MacGibbon & Kee published much of his drama criticism, after his death, in *Theatre*; but probably it was his *Shaw*, containing all his reviews of the G.B.S. plays, many of them written about the first performances at the Court Theatre, with further notices of later productions, that showed him at his best as a dramatic critic. Although he had fresh insights to offer in his later reviews, he never felt he had to retract his original opinions – an example of how he had reached critical maturity at an early age. He had a special admiration for the Shaw plays up, at least, to *Saint Joan*, and the Shaw volume is notable also as the only book he himself actually proposed to a publisher. Although he confessed that the Shaw he had 'admired, and whose plays threw so much light on life for me, died a good many years before 1950', in his forty years as a dramatic critic he had 'written more about Shaw than about any other writer living or dead'.

But what of Desmond's association with Bloomsbury? He came to it, he wrote, through his friendship with Clive Bell and some younger Cambridge fellow 'Apostles', and through his 'introduction into the home-life of Miss Vanessa and Miss Virginia Stephen'. Bloomsbury was never his 'spiritual home'; it had been rather 'what those who cater for sailors (like theirs, my home is a floating one) call "a home from home"'. But he was very much closer to its centre than this implies. Virginia

Woolf's letters and diaries, for instance, are peppered with references to him, mostly affectionate and often admiring: 'I'm not sure he hasn't the nicest nature of any of us – the nature one would soonest have chosen as one's own' (*Diary, I*, p. 241). She herself made more than one attempt on behalf of the Hogarth Press, in 1929, to publish his collected writings in six volumes ('I shall have printers in readiness'), but failed. I suspect that Constant Huntington, Putnam's chairman, in the end secured the contract to publish through his friendship with Lord Esher, who kept a room at the back of his Mayfair house as a refuge where Desmond could do his own writing as well as editing *Life and Letters* – which I think Lord Esher financed.

It seems that Virginia Woolf relinquished the possibility of getting Desmond's writings; indeed, she had already remarked in 1920 that 'being an editor has drugged the remnants of ambition in him' (*Diary, II,* p. 34). She also gave a dinner party in 1921 with a short-hand writer secreted behind a screen to record 'the inimitable quality of his conversation' (*Diary, II,* p. 120), but that plan also failed. I guess the sparkle of his words was lost.

And it was Molly MacCarthy who started the Memoir Club, where Desmond read two papers, published after his death in *Memories* and *Humanities*. Her motive, I believe, was to encourage him to get his reminiscences and stories down on paper. One learns from Richard Kennedy's delightful *A Boy at the Hogarth Press* how often Desmond called there, once leaving a message for Virginia when she was out, so long in the writing that young Kennedy thought it must take him 'a very long time to write his *Sunday Times* reviews'. And Desmond was always prepared to discuss his Bloomsbury friends and their books. Talking of style one afternoon, he said, 'Now Lytton Strachey, he wrote in *clichés*, but *clichés* of good pedigree.' The endearing chuckle followed, suggesting he was pleased with the term. Perhaps Roger Fry was the one he loved and respected most in Bloomsbury: 'The most analytical mind that has been applied to the study of the visual arts', he wrote in his account of how they had organized the first Post-Impressionist Exhibition in London in 1910. In the course of persuading the Grafton Galleries to mount the exhibition Roger Fry, as an extra bait, told them that in Desmond MacCarthy they would have 'an excellent man of business' – probably the only time this particular tribute was paid to Desmond! As many will know, the exhibition aroused a furore of controversy and moral outrage, but it was a success, albeit a *succès de scandale*, and to his surprise, as well as his delight, Desmond's share of the profits was £460 – 'such a lump sum as I had never earned before, and would never do again'. After they had chosen the pictures in France the two men, as Roger Fry had promised, went on a short cycling tour before they left, Roger Fry for London, Desmond for Munich and Amsterdam in search of more paintings for the exhibition – a nice earnest of the trust of the one in the other.

With age one tends more and more to refer to so-and-so as 'the last of his kind', but it is impossible to think of Desmond's equal: he was unrepeatable. He may have suffered from a kind of inertia which prevented him from completing the work of fiction his Bloomsbury friends had hoped for, but how hard he worked, always, somehow, making time to read round the subject of a book under review, either at home or in his beloved London Library. His pen-name, 'Affable Hawk', suited him to a T: he wanted to praise but was ready to swoop down on the shoddy or perfunctory. Lord David Cecil wrote in his preface to *Humanities*, 'Desmond MacCarthy was himself an artist. His writing is a model of what critical prose should be. For he was without the conceit that inspires some critics to expect to find readers when they have taken no trouble to make their own books readable.' The good manners that were such a marked characteristic of Desmond the man, in his relationships, whether with a callow young publishing aspirant or the long-suffering *Sunday Times* compositors, were equally present in his writing. He was the greatest intellectual influence in my life, and, here I am, typing this little piece with triple spacing – always his preference.

SOME MEMORIES OF OCTAVIA WILBERFORCE

Leon Edel

HAVE BEEN reading the last volume of Virginia Woolf's diaries (edited, with great wisdom, by Anne Olivier Bell) and in the entry of 10 January 1937 I find myself stirred by a sequence of old memories. They are vivid. The novelist describes a visit she paid with Leonard Woolf to Elizabeth Robins (1862–1952), the Ibsen actress, and her friend Octavia Wilberforce, M.D. (1888–1963) in their house in Brighton, at 24 Montpelier Crescent. Virginia and Leonard sit with Miss Robins in the back parlour – well-polished tables, solid books, a sketch never completed of William Wilberforce, Octavia's great-grandfather, and a china statuette of him (was he in an orator's pose, with his hands in his lapels?). Strange to think that a few weeks later I sat in that same room and saw the same pictures, the same furniture and the bibelots. I was trying to obtain from Miss Robins some of her memories of Henry James and her having played the lead in his dramatization of *The American* in 1891. She was cautious and monosyllabic. Perhaps I was a too-zealous biographical sleuth. But she listened with full attention and promised to look for the manuscript of a one-act play James had sent her and for other materials. She had been the first of the Ibsen actresses in England and I marvelled at her survival into this new time. She was seventy-five and through her faded beauty there shone the deep blue of her eyes which she fixed steadily on me.

The events of that summer in England rise out of the pages of the diaries: my watching in London the Coronation procession of George VI after Edward's abdication; the appearance of Princess Elizabeth and her sister in the gilded coach; my finding actors and actresses who, like Miss Robins, had played in James's plays and my returning to Montpelier Crescent in July to dine with the former actress and the general practitioner.

This time I sat at a highly polished table by windows

that looked out on the Crescent. Miss Robins again fixed her intensely blue eyes on me; and at the other end of the table sat Octavia, M.D., robust and round-faced, looking a little like her famous ancestor. Octavia had been, along with Miss Robins, among the early Suffragettes; and Miss Robins had helped her assert woman's place by having her take a medical degree when women in medicine were rare. Octavia tended to be shy, but listened as Miss Robins evoked, as in a cinema, picture after picture of the 1890s. She was more outgoing this time. The Kentucky-born Elizabeth Robins was still very American, after her half century of England.

After dinner she produced surprises: my early petition had succeeded. She had the missing play; a letter about James from William Archer, the drama critic; photographs of herself in the Jamesian play and the rare printed acting-edition, with some corrections in the text. She also presented me with a short letter written by James to her – 'I thought you might like to own a letter written by him.' I was then twenty-nine, an amateur researcher trying to break away from journalism. Octavia was in her forties. She wore the kind of black dress Virginia describes in her diaries and the same kind of silver jewellery, loops of chain, about her neck. A hearty young woman, without a scrap of make-up, in contrast to the artful re-touchings on Miss Robins's mask of aging.

I never saw Miss Robins again, although we corresponded, and I sent her, many years later, when she was almost ninety, my long-delayed edition of Henry James's plays. I was destined, however, to see a great deal of Octavia Wilberforce (who had been named, she told me, Octavia because she was the eighth of nine children in her family). One day in 1952 I came on the obituary of Miss Robins, who had died at ninety in Brighton. Remembering my visits in Montpelier Crescent, I wrote a letter of condolence to Octavia on the passing of her old and famous friend and expressed the hope that I might now see some of her papers, for I had begun to write the life of Henry James. Octavia answered promptly thanking me for my 'most understanding letter'. As for the archive, there was 'a heap of stuff left', but the will had not been proved, and so the answer to my question was up in the air.

I heard nothing more for some years. In 1958 or 1959 my London publisher, Rupert Hart-Davis, told me that Octavia was speaking of a Robins biography and had wondered whether I would be interested. Still later, word reached me she was trying her own hand on a life of her friend whom she had known for more than forty years. And finally, when I had occasion to go abroad (in 1959), word came from Hart-Davis that she expected me to pay her a long visit.

In due course I received her invitation. She now lived in Backsettown in Sussex. When the will had been proved, it had been found that Miss Robins had established on her land and in her Elizabethan cottage a rest home for 'tired professional women' which Octavia was to preside over – as health officer and administrator. Octavia said she would reserve a couple of rooms in the cottage for me and expected me to stay all summer and help her with her life of Miss Robins. I wrote that my summer was mortgaged to my Jamesian biographical research, but I would indeed be happy to visit. Thus I found myself cloistered with a group of middle-aged secretaries and file clerks. Octavia had built herself a fine cottage next to the rest house and in it were all the memories I had seen before. On the acreage surrounding the dwellings Octavia pastured cows as she had done even when Miss Robins was alive and had abundant supplies of milk, butter and cream for her convalescents. One remembers how in her diaries Virginia Woolf speaks of the 'leech' Octavia and her bringing supplies of lacteal products to the Woolfs in Monks House. Octavia had prepared a special table for us in the dining room where we sat apart from the tired professional women and could converse privately. Her idea was that I would show her how to summarize the materials in Robins's family letters, especially the drama of her early fight with her family in Kentucky when she wanted to go on the stage.

Octavia was very professional about our arrangements. She began our negotiations by saying she would be ready to pay me handsomely for my consultations and pulled out a large chequebook. I could live on in the house and enjoy the good food and the cream and milk etc. while I worked. In my private annals I have always called this the 'case of the captive biographer'; only I avoided captivity. I knew that if I accepted a sum at this moment I would be contracting for vast and long services. I told her I could stay for only a fortnight; that I would take the measure of her task and charge her only for the work I did. 'You can't read all that material in a fortnight', she said. I replied I was an old hand at absorbing archives, especially when I knew my personae, as I did Miss Robins.

So I set to work. Every morning I worked in Octavia's private cottage. I used to see her from the window, seated proudly on a little tractor she drove through the cow pastures. She wore corduroy slacks and a nondescript rough jacket and looked like any farmhand – with one exception. On her head, jauntily set, was an off-the-face hat, decorated with artificial flowers, her one concession to femininity while on the job.

Near Octavia's cottage was a small neat shed which, she told me, contained all of Miss Robins's papers. It was securely locked and I felt like Henry James's character in *The Aspern Papers* who wonders whether he shouldn't break such a lock and make off with the papers. Octavia played a cat-and-mouse game with me. She brought me individual papers from the shed; and occasionally as a dividend a Henry James letter 'I might be interested in reading'. I was patient, but I knew from my publisher that, like the cream she separated from the milk on her farm, Octavia was selling off parts of the archive – some of the James letters, some Oscar Wilde letters – in order to bolster the finances of the rest home. When I told her that no biographer would want to work with such a dispersed archive, she answered she was only interested in the early years of Miss Robins. Her biography already had its title: *The Making of an Actress*.

At the end of the fortnight I gave her an outline for the biography she proposed to write; and I set a nominal sum as my fee for the work done. I would have liked to have more material for my own biographical enterprise; but I promised future visits, and hoped I could some day see some of the papers sequestered in that enticing shed. I was very fond of Octavia; she was a good-hearted energetic spinster of the old school, happy with her brood of women and the young cow-girls she hired. She sat on the County Council of East or West Sussex. Literature was obviously a mystery to her. She was a concrete, pragmatic individual – a woman who believed in 'getting things done'. The life of the imagination was a strange world to her. I knew also she would never get her Robins biography done. She wasn't a biographer.

I did get a very fine dividend for my work. One day, shortly after I arrived, Octavia appeared in a white dress, another off-the-face hat, and said we were going to have tea with Leonard Woolf. He wanted to meet me. He was on the board of the 'rest home' and was interested in the archive. Nothing could have pleased me more. I knew his work; I had been reading Virginia since my youth and had written about her in the Twenties. We had our first meeting at Monks House and there were subsequent visits and also lunches with Woolf in London. Sometimes Leonard came over to Octavia's for lunch, and sometimes he, rather than Octavia, met me at Haywards Heath when I visited.

Leonard Woolf and I talked of many things on this and subsequent occasions – of Duncan Grant and Vanessa Bell, when I looked at the art work in Monks House; of Virginia's writing habits; of Buddhism, which he had studied in Ceylon; of animals, and especially dogs and cats. He had a cat which had given birth to a misshapen kitten and I remember Leonard's tenderness to the tiny creature which he said couldn't live very long. I remember also his severity to a dog he was training. The strong disciplinarian was always manifest in him. Beneath his surface urbanity there lingered old angers and frustrations which he carefully controlled; he didn't suffer fools gladly. He was the rare individual who refuses to accept half-truths with which we content ourselves. The harsher side of his nature was tempered by his need to see all sides of every question and his unshakeable belief in truth and justice. I was fond of his worldly-wise sayings as he busied himself in the kitchen that first time and gave Octavia and me tea. Later he walked us through the garden and showed me Virginia's work room on the edge of the long meadow, and his tropical plants. In the garden he suddenly bent down and picked up the long tendrils of a fig tree that concealed Stephen Tomlin's bust of Virginia. It was as if I had suddenly seen her ghost – there was her face, as large as life, and her stony gaze into a distance beyond our reach. We talked also of Miss Robins's papers and Leonard, much amused, described how she could throw nothing away: he had found in the archive receipts for soda water bottles from the 1890s.

I wanted to ask Leonard whether Virginia Woolf had been exposed to any forms of Freudian psychotherapy. The Woolfs had published Freud. Virginia's brother was an analyst. But somehow, through perhaps excessive caution, I hesitated to bring up the question of her suicide. I should have been bolder. Octavia however brought up the subject on one occasion after we left Monks House and returned to Backsettown. She told me, what is now common knowledge, that she was the last person, of those who knew her, to see Virginia alive. The novelist had come to her consulting room just before she ended her life. Leonard, knowing Virginia's hatred of doctors, had urged her to consult Octavia who was after all a friend – and a woman – and not of the tribe of insensitive males who had treated her down the years. Octavia had examined her in the usual way of a general practitioner (she had no knowledge of psychiatry), heart, lungs, blood pressure, and told her she was in decent health. They seem to have talked a bit about her melancholy and Octavia seemed quite pleased that she had been as we now say 'supportive' – in other words she had produced her habitual bedside manner and provided 'understanding' and empathy. I had a feeling, as I listened, that Octavia had, in her brisk literal professional way, touched all the wrong chords. She had been, in her own way, as inept as the earlier doctors and later, when I read some of her letters to Elizabeth Robins about this consultation (Miss Robins had been in the United States during the War), I felt that perhaps what Virginia had needed was the opposite of compassion. Octavia had fallen too much into Virginia's mood; and what had been required (we may speculate) was firmness and confrontation – in some way a conveying to the distraught woman that she was contemplating an awful solution. She needed to be shocked out of her crumbling selfhood into the world of reality. Instead, Octavia offered her the usual old-fashioned medical bedside manner. Virginia could see through it, and it must have made her feel more helpless than ever. If we do not know all the talk that passed between Octavia and Virginia, we know that the latter left the doctor and drowned herself.

Below her surface self-assurance, Octavia must have been shaken by the outcome and her failure to be helpful. However, she had been a practitioner too long to allow the vicissitudes of a day's work to upset her equanimity. I saw that in abundance during those wonderful early mornings in the clear air of Sussex when she sat on her little tractor and meandered triumphantly through the pastures, ruling her bovine empire and wearing her little crown of artificial flowers on her off-the-face hat.

3 CHARLESTON

‘Cerlocestone’ appears in Domesday Book (1086). In 1316 the name was written as ‘Charlacton’. By the eighteenth century, on maps and plans, the present spelling had emerged.

Early in the twentieth century Charleston Farmhouse had been a boarding house. In 1916 it became the home of Vanessa Bell and Duncan Grant. After Duncan Grant’s death, in 1978, the Charleston Trust was formed, with the primary aim of restoring and preserving the house and grounds and opening them, for a season each year, to the public.

TOWARDS CHARLESTON

Anne Olivier Bell

My first exposure to what might be called the Charlestonian decorative manner came when I was about thirteen. We lived in a tall stucco house overlooking the ferry at Twickenham; Duncan Grant's mother lived in a brown brick house behind high garden walls near the station. My step-mother Rosalind used to play piano duets with Mrs Grant (whom I never saw), and bring home wools and canvas and designs to embroider in *petit point*. In school holidays my step-sisters and I were pressed into this service while my father or step-mother read aloud to us. The particular designs I remember were by Vanessa Bell and were oval insets for the backs of chairs – Omega-type caned chairs – enclosing a white vase of full-blooming flowers before an open window. The rich and bright subtlety of the colours – the dirty yellow, rose madder, the sky-blue sky – made a deep impression on me. The finished chairs – they are now in the dining room at Monks House – were exhibited in the Cooling Galleries at the top of Bond Street, and we were taken there to see them; I felt immensely proud of my participation. I must have seen paintings by Duncan Grant there too, perhaps the first *modern* paintings to seize my eye (we were Old Master people), and my eldest step-sister and I, inspired by the examples of his art, set up a white vase of bright tulips on a window-sill to paint in oils – a thrilling treat to a child hitherto restricted to the inevitable box of Winsor & Newton's water-colours; it had looked so easy, but my attempt to paint a Duncan Grant was a dismal failure.

That was my nearest contact with these admired and fabled artists until 1937, when, having finished my studies at the Courtauld Institute (more Old Masters), I went to Paris for the first time, and spent a lonely month conscientiously tramping the museums and galleries and buildings and exhibitions. Just before returning to England I went once again to the *Chefs-*

d'Oeuvre de l'Art Français and there ran into Igor Anrep – whom I had once met at a party – with his painter friends William Coldstream and Graham Bell. They commandeered me, and I was a willing conscript, for I was starved of companionship and theirs was wonderfully enjoyable. They took me to see Boris Anrep at work in his studio in the boulevard Arago; he gave us all dinner at a Russian restaurant where the waiters addressed him as Little Father. I was taken to meet Helen Anrep, staying at the Hôtel de Londres in the rue Bonaparte. As we were all descending the stairs from her room on the way out to dine, she held us back; in the hall was a rather shabby group of people, three of whom appeared to form a protective bodyguard to the fourth, an infinitely sad, grey lady. She was Vanessa Bell, whose elder son, as I knew from my then obligatory reading of the *New Statesman*, had recently been killed in Spain. The others were Duncan, Angelica and Quentin. I observed them with reverent curiosity, as they gathered determination to sally forth.

After this I got to know Helen and her *protégés* very well; she was a great supporter of the School of Painting and Drawing they had just opened in Fitzroy Street, which soon moved and became better known as the Euston Road School; and, though I now had a half-time job at the Courtauld Institute in Portman Square, the centre of my social world shifted east from art historians to artists. Duncan and Vanessa sometimes taught at the School – and Quentin and Angelica, I think, painted there – but I never met any of them. Helen always impressed upon me what a fiercely *private* person her great friend Vanessa was, but it was obvious that Duncan was not – he was often to be seen irresolutely stepping down Rat's Alley (as Charlotte-Fitzroy Street was called by my friends) stopping to talk to one person or another. I saw them all again, in the large back studio of the School over the pin-table saloon in the Euston Road, on the occasion of Sickert's lecture there on 6 July, 1938. They had all lunched together and were rather merry, particularly Clive Bell, who introduced the old man and, to his discredit in my eyes (my first sight of him), laughed behind his back at his vagaries and apparent confusions. Sickert was to me a noble figure, in his morning-coat and trousers of bright ginger Harris tweed, collarless French blue workman's shirt and carpet slippers, and was no object for mirth.

Early in the War – the phoney war, when nothing seemed to happen (the Euston Road School had closed down), and Duncan and Vanessa had settled themselves at Charleston – they lent their Fitzroy Street studios to Victor Pasmore, Bill Coldstream and Graham Bell. I don't think they lived there, but used to paint there, and eat there, and talk there; and I was sometimes there too. Those studios seemed to me magical, mysterious caverns, full of grey dust and dusk and the smell of paint, canvases and shabby sat-in armchairs, clumsy colourful pottery and Pither stoves, wine bottles and dying flowers and bits of patterned cloth. But the painters were bit by bit sucked into the war machine (from which Graham did not emerge), and I was too.

When it was over, and when I had finished controlling Germany and then trying to control my work in a publisher's office, I joined the staff of the Arts Council Art Department. In 1950 preparations for the Festival of Britain were very much to the fore. The Art Department set afoot a scheme to encourage painters, restricted by wartime shortages of materials, to stretch themselves, and paint *big* pictures; to which end canvas and paint were to be supplied to a selected sixty painters. At a party given by Helen Anrep she at last introduced me to Vanessa Bell – great trepidation on my side – and I was overwhelmed by her unexpected affability and entranced by the beauty of her voice and smile. I was even more overwhelmed when she said that Helen had suggested that I might agree to come for a weekend to Charleston and sit for her – she had to paint this large picture for the Arts Council exhibition and it was so difficult to get models in the country; she would be very grateful. What could I say?

So I went to Charleston in June 1950 – and that began a new chapter in my life which is not yet finished.

BLOOMSBURY HOUSES

Frances Partridge

An empty house is in one sense merely a shell – but, shells have their own beauty, and also, speaking personally, I am more than glad that Haworth Parsonage, Rydal Mount and Yasnaya Polyana (to take three at random) have been preserved to give us their richly stimulating impression of the lives of the Brontës, Wordsworth and the Tolstoys respectively – for I find they linger in my mind like a picture or a cinema film perhaps, and have a certain quality of indelibility possessed by few biographies. The fact is that the connection between a house and the individuals it has fostered is a unique and potent one.

So naturally students of Bloomsbury want to come to Charleston. But all Bloomsbury didn't live at Charleston; nor did the Bells and Duncan Grant live here *all* the time. What of the other houses that sheltered their friends, and were in different ways connected with it? And what, above all, of that eponymous district of London where they so often forgathered? I shall try to give some sort of answer to these questions, and say a little about Charleston's relations – those other houses (and their life-styles) linked to it not so much by geography as by friendship and common interests and values. Those I have in mind are Tidmarsh Mill House, Monks House, Ham Spray and most of the north-east side of Gordon Square. I shall begin with the last, for it was chronologically the first, and since the ground is well trodden I will confine myself to my own recollections.

When Vanessa bought 46 Gordon Square in 1904, she set going a process of gradual but thriving colonization, which I myself only came in contact with a good deal later, in 1921. This was the year when I came down from Cambridge, and took a job as accountant, delivery girl and dogsbody in Francis Birrell's and David Garnett's bookshop, situated just off Gordon Square, and built to a more or less matching architectural pattern. By this time several houses in the square were in occupation by those who soon became the chief – I might almost say the *only* – customers of our shop, which somehow failed to look enough like Bumpus or Hatchards to invite the casual passer-by. But such visitors as we had were extremely interesting and lively, and the talk they obviously so enjoyed was brilliant and amusing; so that if I happened to be sitting at my desk in the corner struggling to make the accounts meet, even when Frankie or Bunny had failed to enter items on the till, I forgot all about double entry and listened enthralled. At this time I was only what botanists call a 'casual' in Gordon Square. I didn't pull up my roots from my mother's house in nearby Brunswick Square and qualify as a 'denizen' until Ralph Partridge and I finally threw in our lot together and rented the first floor of No. 41 from James and Alix Strachey some four years later. I could never imagine why they let us have the splendid rooms on the first floor, since (both being psychoanalysts) they needed the second floor for their consulting-rooms, and had to make do with the Yonghy Bonghy Bo simplicity of those above to live and sleep in themselves. I really concluded they must *like* discomfort.

On a first meeting Alix and James might strike one as aloof, but this impression resolved itself into a combination of detachment, respect for the views of others and extremely good manners. Alix loved argument, however, and used to support the most improbable propositions on pedestals of the purest logic, untouched by knowledge of the world. James was much more emotional; he felt deeply about causes and heroes (like Freud, Mozart or Lytton) and disagreement merely turned his small round face pink beneath his silky white hair. I think with deep affection of them both, gratitude for the help they quietly gave Ralph and me in welding our lives together, and delight at the memory of their flashes of eccentricity and hilarity. Their patients were something of a worry, though. One might come home to find a desperate-looking, white-faced individual leaning against the Square railings, trying in vain to summon up courage to ring the door-bell. And another of them, described by James as 'refractory' and 'threatening', caused him to take Ralph aside and beg him to be ready to dash upstairs to his rescue at the sound of a thump on the floor above us with the walking-stick he kept beside him for the purpose.

James had also undertaken, and was carrying on upstairs, the stupendous task of translating the *Complete Works* of Freud into English. No wonder that he became practically blind in one eye. I volunteered to take the index off his hands, for I was eager to help; but if you want to go raving mad I recommend indexing twenty-two volumes full of abstract words like 'unconscious' and 'repression'.

Next door for a while lived Oliver Strachey and my great friend his daughter, Julia. Their alliance was the product of *force majeure* and not made to last; but while it did they got considerable amusement from each other's character and behaviour – and probably exasperation as well. During some of the evenings we spent together we would be treated to an unscripted knockabout turn, reminiscent of the dialogue between two comedians at the Palladium; others passed in quiet relaxation, playing word or acting games perhaps, with Angus Davidson, one of the Cambridge boys from No. 37, or chatting while Angus did his *petit point*.

No. 50 had a shifting population, among them Adrian and Karin Stephen, Arthur Waley and his consort, jet-black-haired Beryl de Zoete, of whom it was whispered that she 'came down from Oxford before the Boer War'. (I leave you to work *that* out.) Here too Clive Bell had his comfortable bachelor flat surrounded by his fine library, French pictures and decorations by Duncan Grant. At Charleston he habitually wore old clothes and spent his time reading, writing, walking, and perhaps shooting something 'for the pot', as he called it; but in Gordon Square he satisfied his strong social and amorous leanings and considerable skill as host, the secret of which was that he liked his guests to shine, and that food, wine and conversation were all equally good. I doubt if he was a feminist, but I took it kindly that he always offered me a cigar after dinner. It was usually accepted.

There were parties, too, at No. 46, the Keyneses' house. These often included an elaborate entertainment: for instance a revue based on a topical *cause célèbre* but thinly disguising a satire on Bloomsbury, the hero and heroine, so far as I remember, being called Scrodger Pry and Clarissa Dell. I took part in this production, along with Barbara Bagenal and Bea Howe, in a diminutive male chorus dressed in white ties and tails, while our three strapping 'female' companions were Dadie Rylands and the Davidson brothers, in evening dress and chokers of giant pearls. Maynard and Lytton closed the proceedings with their famous performance of the Keynes-Keynes.

A very different world was hidden behind the front door of No. 51, where Lady Strachey lived with a changing selection of her children, including Lytton at times. The matriarch was monumental in more ways than one, as solid and rugged as a Rodin sculpture. A board in the hall told one who was IN and who OUT, and the maid wore a white cap and apron. It was recognized that none of the family could do a thing for themselves, so on servant's day off some member of the younger generation – probably Janie Bussy or Julia Strachey – had to come to their aid (if necessary by train) and switch on the gas stove in which the evening meal had been left ready – a feat no amount of higher education had fitted Pippa, Marjorie or Pernel (Principal of Newnham) to perform.

The ambience of Gordon Square, as Lytton noted in a letter to Virginia, was very like that of a Cambridge college, and this made it exceptionally pleasant to live in, with seclusion when wanted and congenial company at other times; with strollers or even picnickers in the Square gardens, which took the place of Quad, and where one might watch or take part in a game of tennis, fortified by the addition of Raymond Mortimer from Gordon Place, say, or Frankie Birrell from the bookshop. The latter was a better player than might have been expected from his sometimes scruffy appearance. He had learned to hit a ball at Eton, but was inclined to burst into giggles every time Arthur Waley greeted a shot that was palpably 'In' with a quick, flat 'Out'. Arthur's special technique for dealing with embarrassing facts also appeared on London's ice rinks where he and I sometimes went together. I remember an occasion when the band struck up a waltz: he seized me round the waist, but as we neither of us had the faintest idea how to dance on ice we crashed instantly to the ground in an ignominious tangle; yet Arthur remained impassive while I was helpless with laughter.

So obviously desirable a way of life did Gordon Square provide that it seems strange that its pattern should not have been copied elsewhere. Perhaps it has. As time went on the population was increased by the arrival of the Woolves at Tavistock Square just round the corner, in 1924, while in 1925 Morgan Forster became my mother's lodger in Brunswick Square.

I sometimes think of the houses of geographical Bloomsbury as if they formed a key-ring from which hung a number of keys to other establishments. The first key to slip off this ring into my hands opened the door to Tidmarsh Mill in 1924. This was the attractive old Thames valley house found by Carrington in 1917 for herself and Lytton, with the backing and occasional presence of Maynard Keynes and others, but now occupied by Lytton, Carrington and Ralph Partridge alone. It exactly resembled Carrington's well-known picture of it (reproduced on the jacket of her published letters) except that the swans floating on the mill-stream were white, instead of the exotic black creatures she converted them into. I only visited it a couple of times, not enough to get over my first shyness. I found Lytton alarming, partly because he was shy himself, and clearly just as much afraid of being left alone with me as I was with him; and though I was flattered by Ralph's attentions they were quite unlike those of any previous admirers and left me rather bewildered. Then no one had told me that every Strachey absolutely insisted on eating rice pudding at least once a day, so that the meals struck me as having a curiously nursery flavour. The conversation on the other hand was highly sophisticated, combining erudition with obscenity, the latter inclined to develop when paper games were played after dinner. Alternative evening entertainments were readings aloud from Pope or Shakespeare by Lytton (very moving and delightful) or poker played for low stakes. Lytton was kind-hearted and couldn't refrain from reimbursing any needy looking young visitors who lost. But the paper games filled me with alarm, and I remember one in particular, instigated by a young French doctor who was staying there: it was a form of the Truth game (with the answers to be written on paper), and a typical question was under what circumstances, and when, had we all lost our virginities. Being as yet unqualified to reply I was glad to be let off this one. In fact, of the company at that first weekend I found Raymond Mortimer the easiest to get along with, and the walk we took along the towpath together founded a close friendship which lasted until his death.

I shan't describe the next house I went to, which was Charleston. I can only try to evoke the impression I got on first entering the hall as a visitor – the strong feeling of life being intensely and purposefully lived, of animated talk, laughter, brilliant colour everywhere, youth. I don't think I ever felt shy there – there was so much going on, and I soon began to discover what fun it all was. There might have been a play being performed by Angelica and some school friends wearing dresses designed and made by Duncan and Vanessa. Or I sometimes rattled off with Julian and Quentin in a ramshackle little car known as 'the Pet' to swim in the nearest secluded bay; and everyone in the house seemed to enjoy that strangely unpopular but delightful sport – *arguing*. Little Angelica was musical, and I occasionally accompanied her when she sang or played her violin. She was also enchanting, and I was immensely flattered when she referred to me in a poem in the house magazine:

> And then there's Miss Marshall
> To whom we are partial.

Not that I was ever so addressed of course: Clive soon christened me Fanny to distinguish me from Francis Birrell, a great friend of the house. Excellent meals appeared on the large round painted dining-room table. There was always wine for dinner and the breakfast coffee warming on the hob was hot and strong. The family and their friends came down at all hours, somewhat tousled and preoccupied (Duncan's black hair without a touch of grey was a good advertisement for lack of brushing), and usually hurried off afterwards to carry out their various projects, which were to occupy them most of the morning. Clive carried off *The Times* to his library, and the painters went out into the garden – a rampant jungle of tall flowers buzzing with bees and fruit trees bowed down with ripening apples and pears – to collect subjects for a still life.

Only a few miles away, and in frequent touch, were the Woolves at Monks House, which was on the same wavelength but played a subtly different tune. There was electricity in the air, engendered by Virginia's tense and erratic genius, and though the display of lightning was dazzling some visitors felt ill at ease, wondering where the next flash would strike. But Leonard was a powerful influence for calm and order, with his slow deep voice, steady gaze and trembling hands. The lawn was always beautifully mown, his roses and dahlias grew to supernatural size, and his doting dogs obeyed his grumbled commands and affectionate kicks. I remember no animals at

Charleston, but at Monks House they were an important element. Birds, too, were part of the Woolves' life. On one visit I remember that the hall door could not be shut for fear of disturbing a nesting swallow.

And what can I say about Ham Spray – my own much loved home for nearly thirty years? When Lytton and Ralph bought the house jointly in 1924 I was still working at Birrell and Garnett's bookshop, but I used to go down to Wiltshire at weekends and help paint the inside of the house, while Carrington covered doors, furniture and tiles with her delicate decorations, very different in style from the bolder ones at Charleston. Meanwhile Lytton would be lovingly arranging his books in the library shelves made by the village carpenter, over which, for purposes of reference, Carrington had mysteriously but characteristically painted the letters of the alphabet from Z to A. Ralph would be at work clearing away the 'vulgar' round flowerbeds and the superfluous trees from the lawn – they were mostly conifers, abhorred by Lytton – so that a perfectly clear view could be got from the pink Jane Austen front of the house and its verandah to the Downs half a mile away, leaving nothing between that wasn't green – the lawn, the fields and the ilex drooping gracefully over the ha-ha. Everywhere inside the house were piles of catalogues – Lytton's from antiquarian booksellers and Carrington's from seedsmen. There was always at least one cat in residence.

Alas, Lytton and Carrington had a bare seven years in which to enjoy their country peace before tragedy struck, with Lytton's fatal illness and Carrington's suicide. The house seemed so forlorn that it was hard to believe it would recover and even preside over a happy life again. But the thought of deserting it was unbearable to both Ralph and me. We left London and came to live entirely at Ham Spray. The miracle was somehow accomplished and we developed a way of life that was not so much *di*vergent as *e*mergent from the past. We brought up our son there, and our family happiness was greatly sustained by visits from friends, many of whom came from Charleston. Clive was one of our most faithful visitors, often bringing us a brace of pheasants. Julian and Quentin came too, as well as Angelica and Bunny and their four little girls, one of whom was to become my own daughter-in-law. As in Sussex we walked on the Downs, played garden bowls and not too solemn badminton at which Lytton had once displayed an unforgettable style all his own, rather as if swatting mosquitoes, and Lydia Keynes had distinguished herself by not hitting the shuttlecock once. We enjoyed the hot days in a small swimming pool with a disproportionately high diving-board. The mere hint that a local landowner had closed a right of way along the top of the Downs fired Julian's revolutionary zeal to dash off with wire-cutters and destroy it. It was hard to decoy Duncan and Vanessa away from their studios, except to go abroad, but they were specially honoured guests when they came. We owed their last visit, one icy winter weekend, to a fortunate freeze-up which made Charleston uninhabitable. I remember that we were anxious whether we should be able to keep them warm and happy, but I noted in my diary afterwards that they were the 'nicest visitors and the best company we had had for ages'.

After all there were no great differences between days spent at Charleston and at Ham Spray, but, if any existed, it lay in the way we began the mornings. At Charleston, as I have implied, they started – as they went on – creatively. Ralph and I were perhaps unusual in finding getting up and dressing the best time for conversation. It was certainly now that Ralph spouted ideas like Roman candles, it was the time when we both loved propounding theories, analysing characters, discussing books and political issues, cracking jokes. Some visitors even complained of the noise we made talking all the way down the creaking corridor that passed the spare rooms and led to the bathroom.

But, looking back, I believe there were many more similarities than differences. For after all the keys to the two houses had once dangled from the same ring – Gordon Square; and it was there, too, that Ralph's and my married life had begun, as I very often remember.

Those tall Georgian windows still stare into the Square garden between the dappled trunks and dangling bobbles of the plane trees; but I believe the rooms are all offices or departments of the University now, and the tap of typewriters has replaced the chatter and laughter of those *very* far off days.

A CÉZANNE IN THE HEDGE

Quentin Bell

UNLESS YOU are a pedestrian it is almost inevitable that you will come to Charleston by the Lewes-Eastbourne road, turning south towards the hills at a junction known as Swingates. The gates are gone and the little stream which here runs beneath the main road is all but invisible, but the turning is clear and rather dangerous. Having taken it you proceed almost due south, with, on your right, a dense spinney or 'shaw', as we call it in this part of the world, and on your left a hedge surmounting a rather deep ditch. The spinney once contained a hoopoe, the ditch a still life by Cézanne.

Surely there ought to be some little monument, a small obelisk, a pillar or at least a post. After all, there cannot be many other English hedgerows which have actually housed a Cézanne.

It was placed there some time during the evening of 28 March, 1918. It is a small still life laconically entitled 'Pommes'; indeed it consists of six apples upon a table. In the opinion of some critics it is a masterpiece.

Edgar Degas had died during the previous year, leaving a very remarkable collection of pictures by various hands: they were sold by auction. It happened that Duncan Grant saw the catalogue of the forthcoming sale: he came across it in the London studio of Roger Fry, and it occurred to him that some at least of these pictures might be acquired by the nation. He told Maynard Keynes that something ought to be done. Maynard was at that time spending most of his spare time at Charleston. The rest he spent in the Treasury where, as the War went on, he became an increasingly important official: he if anyone would be able to persuade the Government to so eccentric an act as the purchase of works of art. He was greatly taken by Duncan Grant's proposal and, with typical ingenuity, pointed out that our loans to France were running up and we did not know when we were likely to see our money back. We might, he suggested, help the French to redress the balance of payments by purchasing a few masterpieces. He went to Bonar Law, then Chancellor of the Exchequer, and explained matters. Bonar Law seems to have regarded the whole idea as some kind of joke, but he agreed to it. The money was found and, as a result, Keynes and the Director of the National Gallery, Sir Charles Holmes, set off for Paris. Maynard wrote to Vanessa Bell:

> My picture coup was a whirlwind affair – carried through in a day and a half before anyone had time to reflect what they were doing. I have secured 550,000 frs to play with; Holmes is travelling out with us and I hope we shall be able to attend the sale together. The prime object is to buy Ingres; his portrait of himself being first choice; after that the Perroneau. I think Holmes has his eye on a Greco but admits there would be another chance for this. I am fairly sure I can persuade him to go for the Delacroix 'Schwiter'. I shall try very hard on the journey out to persuade him to buy a Cézanne as a personal reward to me for having got him the money, but I think his present intention is not to buy a Cézanne; I have not yet discussed the question of Corot with him.

Two days later he received a telegram from Duncan Grant. 'Do buy Ingres portrait of Self, Cézanne, Corot, even at cost of losing others.'

Holmes and Keynes arrived in a city which was being bombarded by Big Bertha, a vast German cannon; the news from the front was depressing and indeed agitating, the enemy stood closer to Paris than he had been since the Battle of the Marne. As a result the bidding at the sales of 26 and 27 March was timid. It did not become enthusiastic until the Louvre and the National Gallery began to compete for Delacroix's portrait of Baron Schwiter. It went to the National Gallery; so did Corot's 'Claudian Aqueduct', so did eleven other pictures, including four by Ingres (but not the self-portrait), and two by Manet. But alas, Maynard's persuasive powers were exerted in vain on behalf of the Cézanne.

Vanessa was indignant. 'Holmes's purchases are idiotic, considering his chances. He wouldn't hear of Cézanne and in the end didn't spend all the money, but came back with £5,000 unspent and no El Greco, which he might easily have had.'

But Maynard had become excited by the whole business. He began to buy on his own behalf. He purchased a study by Ingres, two paintings by Delacroix and a drawing also by Delacroix, a study for the hemicycle of the Palais Bourbon which he gave to Duncan. This work had an odd history which, I am afraid, is entirely to the discredit of the Charlestonians. For years it hung in Duncan's bedroom. Then, one summer, the Herbert Reads took Charleston, and when they had departed it was missing. Duncan was convinced that it had gone with them; he based this view on Herbert Read's 'infamous' aesthetic views and he was convinced that they had stolen the picture, until, in the course of a conversation with a friend, it transpired that the friend had bought this work for 6d at a furniture shop in Lewes. Duncan then remembered that he had taken the Delacroix to be framed there. He and the shop had forgotten all about the transaction. Eventually, after Vanessa had intervened in an interminable battle of generosity between Duncan and the friend, he got his picture back and was even prevailed upon, rather unwillingly, to admit that the Herbert Reads had not been so guilty as he had supposed.

But Maynard's greatest coup was the acquisition of a Cézanne still life. He returned with it from Paris rejoicing, and, when he reached England, was given a lift in a Government motor car by Austen Chamberlain. Chamberlain deposited him at Swingates; he had more luggage than he could easily manage on the walk up to Charleston, and that's how the Cézanne got into the hedge. When he arrived, to find the Charlestonians eating their dinner and to be greeted with a hero's welcome, Duncan and David Garnett went out and rescued the picture.

'It's most exciting to have it in the house,' wrote Vanessa and, she might have added, to have it in England. At that time Cézanne was not to be seen in this country except in black and white photographs, usually very bad, in *avant-garde* magazines. I suppose he was only just beginning to appear in public collections abroad. The attitude of Sir Charles Holmes, which seems to us so strange, and so myopic, was at that time the normal attitude in the art establishment. If anyone had known, or cared to know, that such a thing had been brought in triumph to Charleston, I suppose it would have been set down as yet another Bloomsbury fad and the general opinion would have been that the picture might just as well have remained where it was.

In later years, the great question that worried Lydia and her friends was how to make the collection, now valued at many thousands of pounds, secure. Tilton, like Charleston, is a rather lonely place and it was feared that a gang of burglars might descend and carry everything away. Lydia decided that the best thing was to make practically no repairs to the road. It became a rocky and precipitous switchback of shifting gravel and stagnant water. Every now and then two old men would be employed to fill up the craters with sand, sand which was sucked up by the first lorry that passed – the amount of heavy traffic was now considerable – and cast it over a surface which soon came to resemble that of the moon. Perhaps the burglars were deterred, certainly visitors to Charleston found the going hard; at all events no thieves came. But the police and various anti-burglarious bodies felt that more was needed. A vast bell, a kind of Brobdingnagian bicycle bell painted red, was attached to the side of the house. I never heard it ring and have always supposed that if it did it would bring down the wall against which it hung. The pictures were wired up so that if anyone were to touch them an alarm would sound in Lewes police station; indeed it was believed that even if you were to look at them too hard sirens would discharge their music and a posse of police would come racing out upon the A27. But in fact it was not easy to look at them, for they were so disposed as to be barely visible. The 'policeman's hang', as I believe it is called, consists in skying the more valuable works so they are as nearly as possible out of reach. The result was nearly blank walls with a row of masterpieces tilted against the ceiling. In fact the other rooms of the house became almost as bizarre as the hall, an effect which completed the strange aspect of the entire house.

They have all gone now. They went to King's College, Cambridge, where I dare say they presented an even more agonizing security problem than they did at Tilton. For this and for nobler reasons they have gone on a permanent loan to the Fitzwilliam, so now they will be visible, as Maynard no doubt intended, to the general public. I suppose that the public could have seen the Cézanne when it was lodged in a hedge, but the present arrangement seems more satisfactory.

A TALE OF TWO HOUSES

Robert Skidelsky

THERE IS a Keynes Room at Charleston. It is on the first floor, immediately opposite you as you get to the top of the stairs, and overlooks the pond. Quentin Bell is mildly annoyed at its being called The Keynes Room. He remembers it as his room. I want to explain how it came to be the Keynes room, and why it ceased to be the Keynes room.

As all lovers of Charleston know, Vanessa Bell and Duncan Grant first came to Charleston in the summer of 1916. Vanessa, Duncan and Duncan's great friend Bunny had all been living together at Wissett in Suffolk. In July 1916 Duncan and Bunny were both exempted from military service on grounds of conscientious objection but on condition that they did work of 'national importance'. Their existing work at Wissett did not qualify, since they were self-employed. They had to find paid farm work. It was Vanessa's brother-in-law, Leonard, then living at Asham, near Firle, who discovered Charleston. 'It has a charming garden, with a pond and fruit trees and vegetables, all now rather wild, but you could make it lovely,' Virginia wrote to her sister. 'The house is very nice with large rooms and one room with big windows fit for a studio.' It was available to let, on a sub-lease from Lord Gage, and there was a local farmer, Mr Hecks, willing to employ the two C.Os. Maynard Keynes paid his first visit to 'Duncan's new country house', as he called Charleston, in October 1916. It soon became his favourite week-end retreat.

Maynard Keynes was thirty-three and single. He was a brilliant Cambridge economist and philosopher whose own work of national importance was rather different from that of Duncan and Bunny. He was at the Treasury, the favourite adviser of Reginald McKenna, Chancellor of the Exchequer, and the scourge of Lloyd George. He shared his friends' views about the character of the War. His great friend was Duncan Grant, and it was through Duncan that he had come to know Vanessa intimately as well. The ties of affection between the three were long-standing and ran deep.

The permanent household of Charleston, as Quentin Bell has written, then consisted of 'Vanessa, Duncan, David Garnett, a governess and her lover, four children, including the governess's daughter and nephew, a cook and a kitchen maid'. Although he could only get down at the weekends, Maynard was equally a member of Vanessa's 'family'. He contributed to the rent and expenses of the house. He would arrive on a Friday or Saturday evening, recount his War news, and then stay in bed till lunch the following morning, by which time he would have worked through his Treasury files, leaving a waste-paper basket full of torn up paper. Then there would be time for walks on the Downs and evening gossips. He even became an honorary gardener in a small way, weeding the gravel path methodically with his pocket penknife while kneeling on a small piece of carpet. Bunny Garnett recorded that it would have been easy to tell the length of his visits by the state of the path. It was no doubt on one of his walks that Keynes first discovered Tilton, a ramshackle and rather dilapidated farmhouse further up the private drive on the Gage Estate.

The pattern of life which Keynes established during the War continued after the War. In the first six months of 1919 he was away in Paris as Chief Treasury Representative at the ill-fated Paris Peace Conference which issued in the Treaty of Versailles. He resigned in disgust in June 1919 and spent August and September at Charleston writing his *Economic Consequences of the Peace* which made him world-famous. He breakfasted at 8 a.m. and wrote in the Keynes Room until lunch time. After lunch he read *The Times* and gardened until tea. On 3 September he wrote to his mother that he had managed 'to keep up my average of 1,000 words fit for the printers every day, seven days a week . . .' There's a photograph taken by Vanessa of Maynard at Charleston that summer in a floppy white hat and a remarkably crumpled suit. He was more than ever a member of the family. He became godfather to Vanessa and Duncan's daughter Angelica. He invested their money for them. In March 1920 the three of them went off to Italy on a holiday. With the dramatic fall in the value of the lira, and with Maynard also making pots of money for all three of them through his currency speculations, he informed his companions that spending was more than a pleasure, it was a duty. They went on a shopping spree, buying over £300 worth of furniture and fabric. (Some of the furniture can still be seen at Charleston.) When they got back to England they discovered they were ruined. It was on this Italian visit that there occurred the incident at I Tatti which was recalled by Duncan Grant in a Memoir Club paper. They had all gone to spend a few days there in April as guests of Bernard Berenson, who had mobilized Florentine society to meet the world-famous economist. At a grand dinner party given in Keynes's honour by the American connoisseur Charles Loeser, Duncan Grant, mistaken for Keynes, was closely questioned about the reparation clauses of the Treaty of Versailles, while Keynes, posing as '*il pittore* Grant', gave his expert opinion on his host's Cézannes. His hosts were not, apparently, amused when the mistake, which developed into a prank, was discovered.

Keynes was once more in occupation of the Keynes room in August and September of 1920, revising his *Treatise on Probability*. Despite his business losses, he was clearly in a relaxed and amiable mood. Lytton Strachey, visiting Charleston in early September, found the company 'its usual semi-fictional self: Duncan and Vanessa painting all day in each other's rooms, Pozzo writing on Probability, on the History of Currency, controlling the business of King's and editing the *Economic Journal*, Clive pretending to read Stendhal, Mary Hutchinson [Clive's mistress] writing letters on blue note-paper, the children screaming and falling into the pond'. Maynard had started an experiment in time by setting all the clocks back one hour, to what end I haven't been able to discover. The servants rebelled, and refused to wind up the kitchen clock: as a result they had no time at all. Clive went on living and eating according to normal time. 'How mad they all are', Lytton wrote to Carrington. 'The result is extremely Tchekhovesque. But luckily the atmosphere is entirely comic. Everyone laughs and screams and passes on.' Keynes always had his critics in Bloomsbury, and a less benign picture of him was jotted down by Virginia Woolf, who also visited Charleston from nearby Monks House in Rodmell later on that September. She had:

> a vivid sight of Maynard by lamp light – like a gorged seal, double chin, ledge of red lip, little eyes, sensual, brutal, unimaginative. One of those visions that come from a chance attitude, lost so soon as he turned his head. I suppose though it illustrates something I feel about him. Then he's read neither of my books.

There is some foreshadowing here of later estrangement. There was a grand, worldly side to Keynes which Bloomsbury rather despised. Of all the members of Bloomsbury he was least endowed with aesthetic sensibility – though he worshipped artists, made an art of economics and applied artistry to public life.

The last summer Keynes spent at Charleston was that of 1921, and he was once more writing a book – *A Revision of the Treaty*. In October he returned to Cambridge; Charleston was shut up and Vanessa, Duncan and the children left to spend the winter in St Tropez. There on 22 December, 1921 Vanessa received a bombshell in the form of the following letter from Maynard.

> Loppy came to lunch last Sunday, and I again fell very much in love with her. She seems to me perfect in every way. One of her new charms is the most knowing and judicious use of English words. I am going to the ballet tomorrow, and am asking her to supper with me afterwards at the Savoy.

Loppy was, of course, the Russian ballerina, Lydia Lopokova. Keynes had first met her in the autumn of 1918, when she appeared in London for the first time with the Diaghilev Ballet and made a tremendous impression in *The Good-Humoured Ladies* and *La Boutique Fantasque*. She then 'disappeared' mysteriously for two years, re-emerging in 1921. When Keynes fell in love with her again she was dancing the Lilac Fairy in the lavish Diaghilev production of Tchaikowsky's *Sleeping Princess* at the Alhambra. Duncan and Vanessa were puzzled by this turn of events, since Maynard had never been interested in women, but not unduly alarmed. They knew Lydia, too, from the 1918–19 season. They assumed that Maynard would make her his mistress and keep her out of the way, much as Clive did with his mistresses. At first, they sensed no rupture in the well-established pattern of communal living – at Charleston and Gordon Square in London. But letters from Maynard soon revealed he was hopelessly in love and intended marriage (Lydia was already married, but estranged from her husband). They advised 'flight to India' – where Maynard was due to go as a member of a Royal Commission. He cancelled the trip to be with Lydia. What is worse, he installed her at Gordon Square, and virtually left Vanessa to look after her, on her return to London early in 1922, since he was away for most of the week in Cambridge.

Lydia Lopokova was not, and could not be, one of Bloomsbury. She came from a different world, was an entirely different type of person. Yet from the start Maynard insisted that she should be fully accepted as a member of the Bloomsbury family; that she should become part of his life with Vanessa, Duncan, Clive, Virginia, Leonard *et al.* Vanessa and Clive would not have it; and perhaps Lydia did not want it either. The general impossibility of what Maynard wanted transcended personal likes and dislikes. When he proposed to spend the summer of 1922 at Charleston as before but this time with Lydia, Vanessa put her foot down. On 19 May, 1922 she wrote to Maynard:

> Clive says he thinks it impossible for any one of us . . . to introduce a new wife or husband into the existing circle for more than a week at a time . . . Duncan and I feel that the whole matter ought to be faced . . . Don't think however that what I say is any criticism of Lydia, it isn't. We feel that no one can come into the sort of intimate society we have without altering it . . . I can't offer any solution to the summer problem. We would much rather you were at Charleston of course. But I'm afraid you may be forced to choose between us and Lydia.

Eventually a compromise was worked out: Maynard and Lydia spent a few days at Charleston at the end of August 1922, Clive Bell moving out. They spent the rest of the summer in a rented house near Marlborough, where Maynard went riding. The following summer they spent together in a hotel in Exford in Somerset, where he went hunting. Although they were not married, Vanessa and Duncan starting referring to them disparagingly as 'The Keynes'. Two separate households were starting to form, though their lives still were tangled up at 46 Gordon Square, where Vanessa still had rooms and they all ate together. 'My dear, I'm, sorry you have to spend so much of your time with the Keynes,' Duncan wrote to

Vanessa from Charleston on 28 September, 1923. 'It must be terrible for you. You must try to have your separate dining room as soon as Grace returns.' And Vanessa wrote to Duncan from 46 Gordon Square on 8 October: 'We had lunch with the Keynes who were rather triste as usual. Clive came to dinner and I couldn't help feeling horribly guilty in our really very nice little dining room with Grace rushing in and out and delicious food and the thought of the chilly couple with Harland [Keynes's cook] upstairs.' The fixed Bloomsbury view at the time seems to have been that though Maynard was wholly committed to marrying Lydia they had nothing to talk about – hence they always appeared 'rather triste'.

Then in 1924 came a dramatic development. Maynard and Lydia spent a week at Charleston over Easter with Duncan. Lydia fell in love with the Sussex countryside. Maynard discovered that Tilton was available for letting over the summer. He talked about renting it as a permanent summer house. Vanessa was furious. She said she would give up Charleston and go to live in Yorkshire if 'the Keynes' became her neighbours, so deep was her fear that the 'chilly couple', unable to stand each other's company, would spend all their time at Charleston. Duncan wrote from Berlin on 15 June, 1924: 'It's I see rather rather serious the Keynes' taking Tilton, but I daresay we shan't see too much of them – I trust not. Maynard's marriage is a grim fact to face. It will be more grim still if Maynard sees it to be grim before embarking on it, Lord! Lord!' Maynard was delighted with his summer experience. 'This is the most charming house and garden I have yet had,' he wrote to his mother, 'and we are very happy here . . . There is no air like this for work.' Maynard married Lydia on 4 August, 1925. They went to Russia for their honeymoon. On 1 October he told his mother that he had 'definitely decided to take Tilton' on a twenty-one year lease and was embarking on extensive alterations, including 'a new library at the bottom of the yard which looks southwards and Downwards'. His pleasure at acquiring Tilton was enhanced by his discovery that '1000 years ago Tilton was called Telitone . . . and that the tenant was called de Cahagnes – which is the same name as Keynes'.

For the rest of the inter-War years Tilton was the Keynes's holiday home. He and Lydia were in residence over the Christmas and Easter vacations and for two months – August and

September – in the summer. There were further alterations and extensions to the house in 1936, including a new wing and extra bathrooms. The house gradually filled up with ugly furniture. Maynard bought indiscriminately from a favourite Cambridge antique dealer, and from auctions, acquiring forty pieces in a single day, but Tilton sucked it all in. Lydia never had the slightest interest in interior decoration. The glory of Tilton's interior was the pictures – Sickert, Picasso, Braque, Cézanne, Renoir, Degas and Seurat. There was a Degas drawing in the bathroom, a Cézanne in Maynard's bedroom; the William Roberts portrait of him and Lydia hung in the library. But the masterpieces perched, in no apparent arrangement, high up on the walls.

Although Virginia Woolf gossiped about the number of bathrooms the 'great Keynes' had installed, and Tilton, unlike Charleston, boasted a telephone and electric lights, it was never a grand house. The water pipes often burst. A boiler in the cellar pumped hot air into the hall through a metal grille: but elsewhere there were coal fires only, and the damp in Maynard's library made the books curl. The wind belched smoke out of the chimneys and sent draughts swirling round the landings. Despite such inconveniences, Maynard and Lydia were wonderfully happy. The scents and noises of the countryside enchanted them. They were far from heroic walkers, but would totter round the fields and woodlands for a couple of miles before falling exhausted into their waiting Rolls-Royce, with their gardener Edgar Weller at the wheel. 'What a melody of a morning,' Lydia wrote one early March, 'music in the air, smells of strength and softness, one squeaks, stretches and blinks in perfect bliss.' There were the long summers when, weather permitting, Lydia could sunbathe naked in some secluded corner of the garden, while Maynard scribbled away on his world-shattering tomes in the loggia. In 1935 Maynard started farming: he and Lydia took squealing pigs to Lewes market in the back of their Morris Cowley.

Although Tilton was only a couple of hundred yards from Charleston, the two households pursued their ways without much reference to each other. Nor did the Keyneses see very much of the Woolfs, who lived at nearby Rodmell. Vanessa's fear that Lydia would be dropping in the whole time was not realized. She harboured some deep resentment which Lydia sensed; it made her stay away. Virginia and Leonard admired

Maynard chiefly for his brains – but, with Lydia, 'Cambridge conversation' was impossible. The first time Lydia appears in Vanessa's Charleston photograph album is in 1932 – eight years after the Keyneses first took Tilton. Quentin Bell notes that 'Lydia and Maynard were invited to birthday parties once or twice during the summer holidays and invited the grown-ups in return. Though we sometimes met them on walks both they and we were careful not to drop in uninvited.' There were more formal entertainments at Tilton, at which Lydia and sometimes Maynard performed. 'It was the common opinion of Bloomsbury', wrote Nigel Nicolson, 'that the Keyneses were remarkably economic in their hospitality.' Virginia gossiped to Lytton Strachey on 3 September 1927 about 'a night at Tilton, when we picked the bones of Maynard's grouse of which there were three to eleven people. This stinginess is a constant source of delight to Nessa – her eyes gleamed as the bones went round.' Dinner was followed by a

> brilliant entertainment afterwards in the new Loggia, with a rustic audience. Sheppard [later Provost of King's] half naked . . . was Miss T[ettrazini] to perfection: Maynard was crapulous and obscene beyond words, lifting his left leg and singing a song about Women. Lydia was Queen Victoria dancing to a bust of Albert. What did the yokels make of it?

There are records of occasional unexpected encounters with Maynard and Lydia which reveal how little Charleston saw of them. In August 1930 Vanessa went shopping in Lewes. She wrote to Duncan:

> There we meet the Keynes in their Rolls. Maynard looked incredibly white and fat. I talked to him a little and then he said I must go into a shop – he said you'll find Lydia in there – so I walked in and looked in vain for someone looking like Lydia as I imagined her – then I saw a very shabby dingy colourless little creature rather ugly and squat and quite insignificant not even noisy in a corner buying very cheap ugly garden gloves. She seemed to me to be very cold and stiff with me . . . so I did my shopping quickly and left them.

And on 6 August, five years later, we find Vanessa writing this to Duncan Grant.

> We went to tea with the Woolves today. When we arrived I saw through the window someone was there, an elderly man with grey hair and very stout looking rather like a Duckworth I thought, but I couldn't be sure – and when we got in it was Maynard! Really he has changed even in the last few months it seemed to me – Lydia also I thought looking *very* plain and middle aged. No doubt they returned the compliment, but Maynard surely shouldn't look so much older and coarser than Clive, Leonard or you – I think it's owing to his greed which is really colossal and slightly revolting, for its not really a discriminating greed. He simply likes masses of cake as far as I could see. They stayed all the time we were there. We sat outside Virginia's new hut which makes rather a good sitting out place for a hot evening and had quite amusing conversation, stories about Tom [Eliot] and such like, but of course all very general and impersonal really. I feel miles away from the Keynes' now – I think Lydia doesn't like me to have any reference to the past with Maynard – even allusions to the Via Margutta I felt were mal vu. Sometimes he looks as though he still had moments when he remembered another state of things, but it is always swamped by Lydia. Well, I suppose one might easily resent old friends and their attitude, but Maynard has lost all his quickness and charm I think – they are of course very full of the Cambridge theatre and Lydia's production of The Master Builder.

These glimpses give an incomplete picture. Some underlying affection survived, particularly between Maynard and Duncan. And all sorts of contacts remained – through painting, the theatre, ballet. Maynard never lost touch with the younger generation, particularly Julian and Quentin. But the breach occasioned by the events of 1922–3 was never quite healed. Maynard died at Tilton on Easter Sunday of 1946; Lydia went on living there till she entered a nursing home in Seaford in 1977, increasingly infirm and eccentric, tottering down the road wrapped in headscarves and Maynard's old pullovers. Vanessa and Duncan continued at Charleston, Vanessa till her death in 1961, Duncan till 1978. To the third generation at Charleston, the children of Vanessa's Quentin and Angelica, Tilton remained mysterious and out of bounds. Vanessa's references to

Lydia were snooty; Lydia always waved in a friendly way, but never asked the children into Tilton. At the age of ten, Henrietta Garnett, greatly daring, broke the embargo, by marching boldly up to Tilton and knocking at the front door.

> She was tiny [wrote Henrietta]. Although I was only ten (and, even now, am not a tall person) I was taller than her. She was wearing a surprising amount of clothes for such a warm day, and around her head were bound a great quantity of scarves. She looked rather like an old tea-cosy, except for her feet, which were delicate and beautiful, and for her hands which were very graceful.
>
> We took to one another like ducks to water. I dare say it seems strange that a little English girl and an old Russian woman should strike up such a friendship. But we did . . . Lydia had a very engaging, child-like streak in her; I was far from being grown-up. She loved to chatter; I adored to listen and ask her questions . . . On this first visit, she offered me a glass of sweet Sauterne and a marron glacé.

And so I come to the latest twist in this tale of two houses. The relationship between the two houses is now considerably improved from what it was in the old days. I now live at Tilton. It has less magnificent pictures, but, I hope, less ugly furniture than it used to; Charleston's splendour is not only undimmed, but is now accessible to thousands every year. The feud between the two houses is now entirely a matter of history, both sad and comic. What gives me particular pleasure is the thought of a new partnership between the two to preserve a unique, and still living, part of our cultural heritage. All the main actors in my story would have been pleased by that.

PICTURES AT CHARLESTON: PAST AND PRESENT

Richard Shone

Visitors to Charleston wonder why the painters surrounded themselves with so many of their own works and why, considering a certain affluence and unusual opportunities, there are not more and better works by their contemporaries. The present hanging of pictures in the house does give, in fact, a slightly lopsided impression of how the walls must have appeared, for example, in the Fifties.

There was always, of course, a preponderance of works by Vanessa Bell and Duncan Grant, particularly of pictures they gave each other as presents or of portraits of the family. (Both are combined in the paintings of Julian and of Quentin Bell by Grant which hang in their mother's bedroom.) And it is true that, unlike their friends Maynard Keynes or Roger Fry, they were not collectors in any formal sense. But their friendships over many years with painters in England and France and their early appreciation of artists whose work was then relatively cheap (Picasso, Matisse, Rouault, etc.) might well incline an alert visitor to think that the painters had missed some golden opportunities. But if we consider a list of the paintings which in 1951 were hanging in the garden room, for example, we can see that they (along with Clive Bell, by then resident at Charleston) were more adventurous than the current impression suggests.

Around the walls were the following (owners in last column):

SEATED FIGURE	Matisse	Lydia Keynes
STILL LIFE	Gris	Clive Bell
HARBOUR (LE PORT)	Matisse	Vanessa Bell
BOY	Sickert	Vanessa Bell & Duncan Grant
LANDSCAPE	Vlaminck	Clive Bell

STILL LIFE	Picasso	Clive Bell
BOATS (water-colour)	Rouault	Duncan Grant

None of these works is now at Charleston, nor are the paintings by Rouault, Derain, Sickert and Marchand which were usually in the dining-room. The dispersal of these and other works came about through the natural processes of inheritance on their owners' death or, in the case of most of the major French pictures, through their value in the saleroom when incomes in the post-War years were looking threadbare. Of the garden room paintings, three belonged to Clive Bell and were among the earliest of his purchases. The Gris still life 'Les Oeufs' (1911) was sold through the Marlborough Galleries to the Stuttgart Staatsgalerie in 1964 and was in the magnificent retrospective in Madrid in 1985. Picasso's 1907 still life 'Pots et Citron' and Vlaminck's landscape 'Poissy-le-Pont' (1909) were both pre-First War purchases, the Vlaminck having been bought at the first Post-Impressionist Exhibition of 1910. The Gris and another Vlaminck, 'Village in Provence' (so far untraced), were chosen by Clive and Vanessa Bell on a visit to the great dealer Kahnweiler in Paris in January 1914. But it was the small cubist Picasso still life of two terracotta pots and a lemon, compact and simplified, that was the jewel of Clive Bell's collection. It had been purchased from a French dealer, probably Clovis Sagot, apparently before the first Post-Impressionist Exhibition and was the first Picasso in any English collection. Clive illustrated it in his 1914 book *Art* and the painting was hung sometimes in his flat at 50 Gordon Square, sometimes in Vanessa's at No. 37 (where it can be seen in a photograph of the sitting room in *The New Interior Decoration*, by D. Todd and R. Mortimer, 1929, plate 21). Before it was sold, the Charleston artists made copies of the painting and Quentin Bell's version hangs in the garden room as a memento of this influential touchstone. Vanessa Bell, also in the Fifties, made a fine copy of the Vlaminck 'Poissy' before it too was sold. She signed it in such a way that, from a distance, one sees only the large V of her first name, confusing further – so good is her version – any unwary spectator. This too now hangs in the garden room.

Of the other pictures on the list, the Matisse of a seated woman had been bought by Maynard Keynes on Duncan and Vanessa's advice from Matisse's Leicester Galleries exhibition –

his first solo show in London – in 1919. It was on loan from Lydia Keynes for a few years and is now in the Keynes Collection, King's College, Cambridge. The other Matisse – also small and sober in colour – belonged to Roger Fry (purchased in 1926) and was left to Vanessa Bell in his will in 1934. It appears in a still life from the Thirties of her London studio (Towner Art Gallery, Eastbourne) and later in several paintings by her of the garden room. The gouache by Rouault was probably acquired from Roger Fry, who bought several from the artist in 1919 in Paris. A gouache head by Rouault was owned by Vanessa Bell also.

In a 1951 inventory of the pictures at Charleston twelve works by Sickert are listed – six paintings, four etchings and two drawings. Of these, one painting and three etchings, including the famous 'Vision Volumes and Recession' of Roger Fry lecturing, survive as tokens of the warm friendship between Sickert and the Charlestonians. The etchings were from a batch given by Sickert to Duncan Grant in 1923 after a very good dinner at the Etoile restaurant in Charlotte Street. Among the oil paintings were two small interiors which Sickert gave to Vanessa Bell. She found them, according to Duncan Grant, 'in the coal hole, very dirty' in Grant's Fitzroy Street studio, previously occupied by Sickert. She told Sickert of her find and was immediately rewarded for her honesty. Both were small interiors of the studio itself, one of them showing two coster girls *c.* 1908 (now in the Government Art Collection). The more substantial painting of a boy, listed above, was a sombre painting of *c.* 1909 or 1910. Duncan Grant maintained that this was Sickert's own son Maurice by his Dieppe mistress Mme Villain. The other paintings included a very dark head of a woman in a hat against a Venetian background and another of a flowergirl leaning over her baskets (now in a London private collection). Both belonged to Clive Bell. Last of the Sickert paintings is a small scintillating oil sketch of three dancing girls in blue on stage; this belonged to Duncan Grant and is on loan to the house. A disputed 'Sickert' was an enormous unfinished canvas of soldiers from the First War period. This too was inherited by Grant when he moved into Sickert's 8 Fitzroy Street studio, along with a fine sofa and a mirror (also unfortunately no longer at Charleston). Expert opinion recently has ascribed the work probably to a student of Sickert's, though

Grant was adamant that it was by the master himself. It was sold in the early seventies.

I said earlier that Vanessa Bell and Duncan Grant were neither of them collectors. But they were certainly acquisitive, with an eye for a bargain or for some unusual work – often anonymous – which struck them as sympathetic. In this way Duncan Grant acquired a seventeenth-century Spanish still life by an unknown artist, which now hangs in the studio. But Grant's most celebrated *trouvaille* was a Poussin.

Walking down a street in Paris in 1921, Grant chanced upon a dark and dirty French sylvan scene with figures, for sale, cheap, in a second-hand shop. He thought it had quality, was reminded of Poussin, and bought it. In later years it hung over the mantelpiece in Clive Bell's downstairs study. Although often referred to as Duncan's Poussin, it was not until Anthony Blunt pronounced on the painting in 1964 that the attribution was made safe. It was entitled 'Landscape with a Man Pursued by a Snake', given a date of *c.* 1635 and assigned a place in a group of works by Poussin on a similar theme. Blunt bought the work from Grant and sold it a few years later at a handsome profit to the Montreal Museum of Fine Arts, an act to which Grant referred with philosophic forbearance.

This brief investigation of 'missing' works at Charleston must not be read as a melancholy story. That pictures come and go is inevitable, and the Charleston Trust has been extraordinarily fortunate in being able to furnish the walls with so much that hung at Charleston over a long period. Outstanding, of course, are the Delacroix drawing, Grant's 1913 'Lytton Strachey', small works by Derain, Friesz, Segonzac, prints by Manet, Pissarro, Redon and Toulouse-Lautrec. We have at least two marvellous pastels by Simon Bussy and representative works by Grant and Vanessa Bell's friends and colleagues Edward Wolfe, Edward le Bas, Keith Baynes, Fred Porter, Henry Lamb and Matthew Smith.

Of the Charleston artists' own works, many good examples were sold in the Sixties and Seventies, reflecting the renewed interest in the artists' work. When I first came to the house, in 1965, a great many pictures had found purchasers at Grant's Wildenstein retrospective of the year before; including his Lady Ottoline Morrell (1913; private collection, London), the early collage 'Caryatid' (*c.* 1913; Manchester City Art Galleries) and a large 1914–15 reclining female nude, sold at Wildenstein to Vivien Leigh (see Christie's, London, 9 June 1989, lot 292). I remember well Vanessa Bell's 'The Mantelpiece' (Tate Gallery), Grant's 1911 painting of Virginia Stephen (recently purchased by the Metropolitan Museum of Art, New York) and Grant's 'Maynard Keynes's Hat and Shoes' (*c.* 1909). This last hung unframed in the studio and was on the wall across from where I frequently sat when Grant painted me. When it passed through the saleroom some years ago, it gave me a pang of sentimental regret. No one in this country thought it worth retaining and I believe it is now in Japan.

CHARLESTON REVISITED

Quentin Bell

VISITORS TO Charleston will have noticed that the big studio on the ground floor is of an irregular shape. Projecting into the garden at the west end of the studio is a small chamber. It existed before the studio was built and was an earth closet. In 1918, when the mosaic was built on the adjoining land, it became a summer house. In 1925, when it was incorporated in the new studio, it served as a store for painting materials and canvases.

But it had another use. There were occasions when that end of the studio was curtained off, the walls were adorned with scenery and props and the *ci-devant* earth closet became our green room. Most summers there was a play at Charleston. Sometimes my brother and I collaborated, sometimes he worked single-handed. He had a taste for long speeches, very long stage directions and social unrest. I had a strange knack for writing any quantity of quite pointless dialogue. Our sister outshone us both by writing an opera. This was performed on the lawn behind the little pond and looked very pretty. It was a pastorale, the music taken, I think, from seventeenth- and eighteenth-century sources. But the libretto was, surely, her own invention. I remember the delight of Dr G.H. Rylands when one of the characters declared:

> And he has a heart so tender
> It would melt an iron fender.

Who he was I cannot recall, possibly Damon who later in the opera behaved like a cad and was reproved in the following manner:

> Damon, demon
> Damon, die.

Which, having been struck on the head with an African knobkerry, he promptly did.

My own first offering was *The Last Night in Old Pompeii.* It was written, with some assistance from my brother and Mr (now Sir) Edward Playfair, in what were supposed to be heroic couplets. Some fragments remain in my mind. Here is the messenger informing the rest of the cast that Vesuvius has erupted (a fact which had hitherto escaped their attention).

Poseidon's trident wakes the startled herds
And sends the mountain top to join the birds.
High in the air the scattered fragments soar,
Resulting from the earth with dreadful roar.

The messenger then alludes to the cloud of volcanic dust which has been released.

Wafted on tender gales this fearful pall
Approaches swiftly to destroy you all.

Not a moment too soon, you may say. But the audience was kind. (I could have wished that it had not at once improvised a spoof Chekhov charade which put my effort to shame.)

I was to need all the kindness that it could find after my next effort, for on that occasion the audience was not only bored but insulted. *Charleston Revisited* was performed for the first and last time about forty years ago. The scene was set in Charleston, in fact on the very spot where it was acted; but the time was about forty years hence, in fact what we now call 'the present'. The characters were a group of visitors to Charleston and a uniformed guide. Christopher Strachey was the guide, Mlle Jane Simone Bussy (Janie played a major role in most of these theatricals) was a tyrannical French mother, Miss Eve Younger was her hapless daughter, I was a very large American lady (a horrific photograph of me dressed for the part is in existence). We were produced by my sister, who was then, or just had been, at the London Theatre Studio.

The guide did most of the talking. He talked about the furniture, and the furniture was the audience. Maynard Keynes was, of course, a safe, Leonard and Virginia Woolf were twin bookcases labelled Fact and Fiction, my father was an eighteenth-century *escritoire*, and so on. The device lent itself to some pretty broad humour which did at least hold the attention of the audience. But we found, in rehearsal, that the play lacked action; the tourists had too little to say and there seemed no way of getting them off stage.

I think it was Angelica who made the brilliant but improper suggestion that everyone should be desperately anxious to go to the W.C. The suggestion was received with joy. It gave some lovely opportunities for dialogue between Janie and Eve and it gave us all some very satisfactory 'business'. Finally, when a notice was discovered saying LADIES, it got us in one ugly rush into that room which had once been a privy.

I was sufficiently imprudent to show the script to a friend, one of those girls who tell you things 'for your own good'. Her comment was that it was a very bad sketch and that it was based upon an absurdity. The absurdity being that anyone should ever want to preserve Charleston.

No doubt it was a pretty bad play; but it does allow me to say that, on one occasion at least, I have been a prophet.

LIFE IN THE KITCHEN AND ELSEWHERE

Angelica Garnett

WAS THERE ever a proper nursery at Charleston? I do not think so, and yet I'm almost sure I didn't always have my meals with the grown-ups. Sometimes in the kitchen with Grace, Louie, Lottie and perhaps others. Hot, steamy and dark, even in summer the kitchen range was alight: Lottie made it roar, manipulating the iron rings in the top. Hungry from our walk we sat at the square table and ate slice after slice of white bread and butter, drinking milk from the farm. Louie sat on the edge of her chair and kept us under her eye: in the dining-room she could do nothing about our manners, but in the kitchen we must behave ourselves. At the same time she was protective; volatile Lottie must not be allowed to alarm us. I loved Louie, but Lottie was more fascinating. She was a foundling, and that was why she was called Hope. She had been left in a cradle on the doorstep of the Hospital, where they had taken her in and looked after her. She had fuzzy hair like a Golliwog's, and her legs were elegant, like those of Mistinguett. Her strap shoes sounded on the kitchen floor almost as though she was tap-dancing in her swinging, pleated skirt. Sometimes her nose looked very red, and she scrubbed it with her pocket handkerchief as though it itched. Where did I hear a rumour that she kept a bottle of whisky in her bedroom? and sometimes lost her temper with violence? When the house caught fire it was she who noticed the smell, and, very excited, ran and told Vanessa. The beam was smouldering and, it seemed, had been burning for weeks. Lottie was a person of extremes; she got up first in the morning to rake out the fire and start it going again, and it seemed as though it melted all the fat off her, and left her, thin and dark, dancing energetically over her saucepans. She was full of laughter, mostly scatty, and strange superstitions jostled in and out of her head, causing Nessa to sigh, after ordering dinner in the morning after breakfast. Having done her best to pour cold water on Lottie's notions, she always discovered that, by the following day, they had returned. One of them was that we liked hot fruit cake, black with raisins and currants and hurriedly iced with thick, soft icing into which she stuck shining red cherries, reminding one of globules of stained glass. Even when we unkindly sent the cake back to the kitchen, saying it was too fresh, we produced only brief discouragement. The following week another would appear, until Vanessa, in some ways the most easy-going of housekeepers, would exclaim at Lottie's extravagance, and discover extra packets of cherries and pounds of currants at the back of the kitchen cupboard.

It was not Lottie however, but an anonymous cook, who came only for the holiday, who overpowered us with jellies. She was the Jelly cook *par excellence*, and discovered in a corner some genteel glass dishes which she filled with the quivering jujube-like mixture in red, yellow and green. Neither lunch nor dinner nor tea was complete without them, and nothing we said changed her conviction that we loved them. We were left with the impression that she had a limited mind – but she must have thought the same of us.

Once I had grown old enough to be allowed to stay up for dinner, each evening became a festive occasion for which, after a day spent getting covered with paint, or mud in the River Ouse, I bathed in the cramped and primitive bathroom, and changed into something which, whatever it looked like, felt like an evening dress. Nessa too changed, and wore long hanging earrings given her by Roger. She looked more beautiful than ever, but her manner, calm and sedate, remained the same.

No matter what Clive did he was always clean – indeed one could only imagine him touching something dirty with hands protected by gloves or a handkerchief. He did not change his clothes for dinner, but brought with him a sense of occasion, a need to find excitement somewhere. I and a friend were the 'young ladies' – what had we been 'up to' all day? He supposed this and that, and with a subtle smile attributed to us all sorts of witty and delightful things we had never thought of. He commanded the conversation, and, having satisfied our looking to be taken notice of, turned his attention to someone else. Perhaps he would call Duncan 'the Colonel', a gambit which enraged Duncan, and made him rub his nose between finger and thumb, trying to think of an adequate answer – an effort which left him laughing, helpless in the face of an attack which seemed to have neither rhyme nor reason. His own contribution to the conversation, always personal, would be an account of some brush with authority in Lewes, or an unforeseen reaction to some well-known work of art, to which he had 'come round', after subjecting it to years of neglect. This would start the sort of conversation that Clive loved, in which he could show off both his erudition and his sophistication, though he was never unmindful of Duncan's originality. There was a deep bond – more than a *modus vivendi* – between them, on which Vanessa, on the other side of the table, looked with a slightly envious but detached amusement. She seldom joined in unless directly appealed to, when, if a work of art was in question, her reactions were almost maddeningly vague. She hated to commit herself, and yet all seemed to her very obvious – her mind was already made up and had been years and years ago.

Julian, partly enjoying things as they were, and partly longing to bring in the revolution and turn everything topsy-turvy, couldn't help introducing politics – local perhaps, but just as red to a bull as any others, indeed more so. Though Clive would try to keep his temper, still he had to have his say, at some length, while Julian fidgeted on his chair in total disagreement, which at length burst forth in a kind of squeal, Julian raising his hand, though not quite bringing it down on the table as a fist. Occasionally Nessa's cool voice intervened . . . but usually the intense emotions were battened down, controlled under hatches: the dinner, the evening were what counted.

It was Quentin who brought a leavening of objectivity into these exchanges; thoughts that had occurred to no one else went deeper, further back, made connections, suave, considered, intellectual and just as erudite as Clive's. Delighted, everyone leant back and sipped their wine while Vanessa carved the bird or helped the syllabub.

After the meal I was sometimes put through a questionnaire on the history of England, supposed to help my schooling, but more often I sang songs to my own accompaniment, while the gentlemen smoked cigars and drank brandy. Sometimes I simply flirted with my brothers or other guests – whatever I did I was outrageously spoilt, my ego outrageously administered to; and that is, probably, the main explanation of my character.

HOLIDAYS AT CHARLESTON

Virginia Nicholson

UNTIL I was eleven we spent part of every summer holiday at Charleston, so anything I write about those times will inevitably have the wallowing-in-nostalgia quality of remote halcyon summer days spent in childish pursuits. Can I assume that most people who are reading this will have visited the house in its present state of resurrection, that they will recognize the rooms and know the names of the people who lived there? They may also have read my cousin Henrietta's essay about her own Charleston childhood in *Charleston Past and Present*, the Charleston guide book. Though she is older than I and thus had a longer experience of time spent at Charleston – certainly she knew our grandmother better than I did, for Vanessa died when I was six – nevertheless many of our memories duplicate one another. When I read her description of being given a coffee-soaked sugar lump by Nessa, it took me back instantly to my own experience. And I remember, as she does, sitting in the studio being painted by Nessa and Duncan, while we told stories to each other. So whilst this demonstrates, I think, Nessa's charming and imaginative relationship with her grandchildren, I shall try not to repeat Henrietta's memories, but find a few of my own.

I was born in Newcastle; when I was three we moved to Leeds. Getting to Charleston from such northerly reaches was a long and tiring journey in those days. We often had to stop and break our journey in Huntingdonshire with my uncle and aunt, Bunny and Angelica Garnett, before ploughing on – crossing the Thames by ferry at Tilbury, on and on southwards until somewhere beyond Tonbridge the first sight of the South Downs rose up like a pilgrim's vision. From then on the three of us (I, my brother Julian and younger sister Cressida), by now tired and thoroughly scratchy, would set up a wail in the back seat of the car: 'When are we getting to Charleston, Mummy? Oh, *when* are we getting to Charleston?' The twists and winds of the A27 (which now looks like an aircraft landing strip) tantalized us as it wiggled past Gibraltar and Stamford buildings; finally, the Bumpy Drive – the bouncy pot-holed mile of track up to the house – and here I duplicate Henrietta's account again with a memory of the curious Babushka Lydia Keynes bobbing down the lane and poking her wrinkly red cheek through the car window to be kissed by Quentin's children. Once the car, driven by my L-plated mother, slithered into the ditch. Quentin set off to Tilton to get help, and I felt great pride when I saw him return, *driving a tractor*, to pull us out!

We arrived at last at Charleston, and arrival meant first of all greeting the dog Blotto, Grace Higgens's blotchy mongrel who lived in a barrel by the back door, with whom I felt a rather uncomfortable affinity because I was told we were the same age. I can remember always making first for the kitchen to see what Grace had been cooking. It was often rock buns or sponge cakes, known to us as 'Grace cake', which she made to a special recipe of her own. Julian and I fought to lick the sponge mixture from the bowl.

The three of us slept in the attic. In one corner was a strange curtained hanging cupboard full of extraordinary dressing-up things; in the other corner was a dolls' house. In the mornings Grace would come and wake us up by drawing the curtains – they were a memorable black stripey chintz with red roses.

Sometimes we stayed the whole summer holidays, sometimes just for a few days on our way to go camping in France. One summer merges into another; all my memories are redolent of the sensual pleasure of the house and garden: the smell of cake and oil paint; musty, booky, pondy scents that wafted through the house, beams of light filled with motes, radiant colours, vibrant dahlias, the resounding clang of the dinner bell, the taste of Marsh's sausages, the texture of lovely slimy crocks of clay in Quentin's pottery, of crunchy mounds of gravel we played with on the front path, the sting of ants (which Nessa called emmets) and of the nettles round the pond, the sploshing of water in the cow trough across the farmyard where we were allowed to bathe.

Nessa, Duncan and Clive preferred to have lunch and breakfast with quiet conversation and newspapers, so when the large and noisy Bell family came to stay we were relegated at mealtimes to the outer studio equipped with a Baby Belling and a sink. Olivier made our lunch there, within calling distance of Quentin's pottery. Beside the door I (aged five) had my shop – a row of little stones and objects I'd picked up in the garden, lumps of chalk or fragments of broken china. I would try and sell them to passers-by, usually my mother – though one day I struck it lucky and sold a pebble to Benjamin Britten.

My brother Julian had one goal to fulfil each summer, and that was to complete a circuit of the pond. Every year the brambles covered our pathway, and Julian would return and methodically set about to clip and hack his way back to the far side. It was like exploring the Amazon jungle. I would follow him. When we finally got to the far side, beyond the statue, we made a nest in the roots of a willow tree full of fascinating woodlice, damp and reedy. Triumphantly we held a tea party in this spot (supplied with Grace's rock buns) for the entire household. For Duncan, Clive and Nessa it can't have been a very comfortable celebration.

Quentin brought us up to be pyromaniacs. We did thrilling things at Charleston that somehow never happened the same way in Leeds. One summer holiday Quentin helped us to construct a wonderful town entirely out of paper, with churches, houses, bridges, all painted and glued together, a masterpiece of town planning, pasted to a sheet of cardboard. We took the whole thing out on to the gravel in front of the pond and ceremoniously set fire to it; it blackened and curled with a glorious rush of flame and was finally consumed in smoke.

Painting of some sort was a constant activity. At Charleston I was taught by Quentin to do *tachiste* pictures. The modish technical nomenclature disguises the abandonment of this art form: you load a paintbrush with dripping poster colour and aim it at a piece of paper – lovely coloured spots, splashes and dribbles are the result. On the paper and everywhere else.

And naturally holidays at Charleston had the added joy of being on a farm. Cressida and I as little girls spent hours gazing deep into the eyes of our favourite Jersey calf. The hens who lived in the granary laid reddish-brown eggs which we helped to collect. Nobody stopped us exploring around the fields, though Cressida and I once had to be rescued knee deep in mud, having lost our boots in a bog. Julian and I followed in Quentin's footsteps and took on the damming project in the stream by Compton Wood – a wet but educational activity.

I think such blissful moments have blotted out most of the sad ones, though certain places around the house still recall to me moments of childish dejection: just inside the walled garden door I sat in the sandpit feeling abandoned. Quentin and Olivier had left me to go on a day trip to Dieppe. But the sadness was transformed into delight when they returned with a wonderful bag of French sweets for me shaped exactly like pebbles. In the courtyard below the kitchen window I stood crying and uncomfortable with wet knickers – a curiously vivid memory! And one evening I crept into the studio, firelit with pools of light from the lamps beside the coloured armchairs. Nobody was there, but in one of the pools of light there was a glass brimming with tomato juice. Greedily I took a guilty sip. It instantly burnt my throat so badly I felt I'd been punished for drinking it. Surprisingly I now find Bloody Mary a delicious drink – it should have put me off for life.

The most terrifying place in Charleston was an almost inaccessible attic full of dusty junk and rotting furniture called the Bat Room. It had no light, and Julian and I dared each other to climb in and, once in, to explore to the far end of its spooky recesses.

I was eleven when we moved to Sussex. By then Duncan was living in Charleston on his own, though he had many visitors. Every Saturday Quentin drove the few miles from our house to spend the day in his pottery, and would often return bringing Duncan to have dinner with us. But Charleston had acquired an air of melancholy and decay, especially after Grace retired. I would walk over there quite frequently and find the house full of strangers. The garden went wild, the pond was covered in bullrushes, the decorations started to peel from the walls. That time coincided with my teenage years. I can remember having a phase when I wanted to learn how to paint in oils, so one February afternoon I set up a palette and canvas in the Charleston drawing-room (now called the garden room) and tried to paint a Charlestonian still life – a lamp, a bowl and the big grey paisley pattern of the wallpaper. My hands perished of cold as I tried to paint, I became numb and disappointed, and the silence of the room oppressed me. The result was a mess and a failure. I felt inadequate, I couldn't copy the past.

Still Duncan himself in old age had such spirit, such an ability to live in the present, that during his lifetime the ghosts of Charleston didn't come out to haunt the crumbly corridors. Even when he was very old Duncan loved to sit up late after dinner at our house, merry and chatting; he could never resist a brandy and a cigar. Once when he must have been about eighty-five we talked him into playing charades. I'll never forget him playing the part of a tourist caught trying to smuggle his pet kangaroo past Customs officials. 'It's only a *very* small kangaroo,' he pleaded.

When Duncan died, the house died, or very nearly.

I love it now; in a personal way seeing the restoration of Charleston gives me confidence; going there on a sunny day brings me so close to my happy childhood, and reminds me of the things I think are important in houses – places to escape to, places to hide, lots of outhouses, unrestrained gardens, a sense of individualized muddle where each discrepant object is bound into a whole by the personality of whoever lives there, and the feeling of a place where people worked alone, creatively, and then gathered around tables and firesides at the end of the day.

THE RESTORATION OF CHARLESTON

Angelica Garnett

WHEN I first saw the film made about the restoration of the house, I was inevitably struck by the fact that the two people who are responsible for Charleston are conspicuous by their absence. This fact, obvious though it is, is brought home, paradoxically enough, by a film which celebrates their gifts. This it does with insight and discrimination, and perhaps it is only for me that the impact of such a film must forcibly recall presences that are no longer there. True, we are reminded of Christopher Mason's film about Duncan, and we see one or two snapshots of Vanessa. But we miss her presence, we do not hear her voice, and as I realize how narrowly she missed being filmed, and how easy a film would have been to make, in spite, probably, of her own protests, I regret the source of inspiration it would have provided.

Had we been able to see her, as we see Duncan, in the act of painting, her brush moving slowly, almost dreamily, across wall or canvas with sensual indulgence, we might have understood something of the spirit in which the decorations were conceived, as well as glimpsing the depth of her concentration. This was not so much intellectual as a state of absorption, almost of trance, all the more remarkable because at any moment she was liable to interruption from the cook, the children or the telephone. We might also see her, suddenly conscious of some omission, lift her hand to her forehead, leave on it a mark of red or blue, and exclaim at her stupidity. Whatever it was that had struck her as wrong – a colour left out or a dribble too much – she would certainly have found a way to adapt or improve the original, and continue what one might call her tightrope act, with serenity.

As things are, however, it is the house that, or – as I was about to say – who, has taken over. It is she who is now the personality, the centre of attention, and of whom, in this film, we have a portrait. She is mysteriously alive, with the life given her by Vanessa and Duncan, and proves to be still full of secrets, like some latter-day Sybil. But because she cannot answer our questions in words, we have to woo her with loving care and put ourselves into a state of sympathetic concentration, hoping to decipher her meaning. We can no longer talk to the artists; it is to the house that we must listen. If the message is wordless, it is nonetheless both potent and poetic and, because it is a question of images, of the mark on the wall, it is there for us to read with our eyes.

One of the reasons why we are seduced by Charleston is its evident fragility, which in itself makes it so different from a national monument, or at least from those other houses which are generally regarded as classic examples of their kind, confirming for us a whole epoch and maybe a whole class of people who, we suppose, lived 'like that'.

Charleston is not a museum piece: it is not a *pièce montée* which has been put into the freezer, waiting for our inspection. It does not tell us anything about a general way of life and cannot be taken as typically English. As decoration, it does not exhibit a fashionable style of the time: it is, rather, a one-off experiment, an example of individualism, pursued for its own sake, certainly not to impress the Joneses or anyone else, nor because it has a moralistic or political message, but because it was as natural for those concerned to express themselves in this particular way as it was to breathe. It is this breath of life the restorers are trying to charm into remaining with us for as long as possible, a task which, in some ways, is made all the more delicate not because we do not know enough about it, but because we know so much. The creators of Charleston inhabited it so recently that it is not so much a question of discovering or exposing their traces as of not obliterating those that remain.

In the case of an Elizabethan mansion or a Queen Anne house, the documentation of its inhabitants is usually sparse and impersonal. If we know *what* they did we do not know how or why they did it, nor which things they liked or hated doing. We have some idea of the style, but little of the idiosyncrasies of their behaviour, and we usually only know how much they appreciated their houses in terms of financial value. The more they spent on them the more precious they were: but how much did they really like them? Probably a lot, but one cannot help feeling that they viewed these things with ineffable simplicity: they had not yet reached the age of self-consciousness.

In some ways *not* knowing these things makes it easier for the restorers, since life does not interpose itself between them and the bare bones of architecture or restoration. The restorer can peel off layers of dirt, burnish the gilding or sand down the wainscot, confident that he is giving back a lost glory, and that when he has finished we shall see before us a perfect work of art, something so perfect, so complete in itself, that we shall be awed into thinking 'Is it possible that ordinary human beings lived normal lives in such surroundings?'

But with Charleston it is not so. We may treasure the building because it is typical of Sussex; but neither is it unique, nor is it an architectural gem. If we want to save the house it is because of the life that went on inside it, expressed in such an extraordinarily individual way. Far from being designed by professional designers and architects who, after finishing their work, went off and designed something else, the house was decorated by those who lived in it and who, over the years, added to their decoration and even changed their style, again and again. It is very different from a house where every corner has been thought out in order to sustain a single idea. This is very satisfactory and beautiful, but it turns out that the opposite can be equally so: Charleston may be an amalgam of different styles, but the impression it leaves on us is benign, restful and holistic. We envy those who lived there for the gay, calm and luminous surroundings, even though these show no apparent homogeneity, and although there is not a straight line or right-angle to be found anywhere.

This is another thing which makes the task of the restorer difficult. He or she can never relax, settle back on the ladder and reproduce a mathematically correct line on a cornice, or replace a worn out piece of wallpaper with a modern reproduction indistinguishable from the old. No doubt the skill required is as great in both cases, but Charleston requires more imagination, more sympathy with the aims of the artists. The restorers have been asked to make a great imaginative leap, a break with tradition, and to understand not only what the artists were trying to do, but what they refused to do. Even more unacceptably, they have been asked to devote their skills to restoring things that were never meant to be permanent.

Looking at Charleston today we are charmed by the gentleness, the softness of the colours and the freedom with which they are handled. These things are no longer shocking, because we have seen a plethora of art books, magazines and reproductions; our visual experience is too sophisticated and we respond to an effect that seems to us wholly natural. It may seem odd to remember, therefore, that Duncan and Vanessa were trying hard not to produce anything that could have been called 'pretty' or tasteful. They were intent on evading the laws of the interior decorator which tend to suppress a spontaneity that, for them, was infinitely more valuable. They did not set out with intent to shock. But if they happened to do so they were not above being pleased, since the ability to shock is proof of vitality. Life, when watered down by good taste, seemed to them not worth having.

But if, at Charleston, spontaneity was rated highly, it did not become an end in itself. Both Duncan and Vanessa had been educated in academic schools, and their response to the immediate sprang from the knowledge and discipline thus acquired. It was a bonus, an overspill from a general effort to liberate their lives, and therefore their surroundings, from all that seemed to them pretentious or dull, everything that still clung to a dead tradition. And at that time the most potent tradition was still that of William Morris, whose traces were everywhere evident and had become, by then, in many contexts, dreary and irrelevant. He himself said 'My work is the embodiment of dreams, one way and another', but his dream had by then lost its urgency and become a sort of safety net protecting the innate conservatism of the English middle classes. Charleston is also the result of a dream, but, one feels, of a more private one than Morris's. Vanessa and Duncan were not didactic; if they had a vision, it was primarily for themselves, they had no intention of preaching to others. Not entirely devoid of social conscience as they were, favourable to the idea of the availability of art and against its being only for the rich, it did not follow that they wanted to impose their idea on the public at large: they were no crusaders.

Morris was a visionary, exalting his strong feelings for exquisite craftsmanship to a level where it became a symbol for a life of spiritual refinement and discrimination. His insistence on moral, political and literary elements was supremely English.

He loved things for their own sake, intent on knowing what they were and why they were there, what their use was and why they had been designed in that particular way. He appreciated them in their context, and when necessary re-created such a context for them, using his enormous practical and historical knowledge in order to do so. It is impossible not to respect such a vision, not to be touched by its innocence and simplicity, its faith in the past. But in some very important ways it embodied exactly what Duncan and Vanessa most distrusted, since what they were looking for was not the knowledge of what a thing is or how to recognize it, in other words a label. Indeed, they avoided such knowledge, searching for relationships, connections that exist beyond it, and that produce something unexpected. Where Morris was a perfectionist they were concerned with the aesthetic of immediacy, with a state of repeated or on-going experiment in opposition to Morris's cult of the past.

In another way also Vanessa and Duncan's attitude to decoration was at the opposite pole to that of Morris. For them Charleston was not an end in itself, so much as an opportunity that had fortuitously presented itself. It was not so much a house to be decorated, and thus made into an entity that might continue to exist on its own into an indefinite future, as yet another canvas waiting to be painted. Their style as painters is repeated on walls and doors, on fireplaces and furniture, which explains why the brush marks remain visible, why accidents are accepted as felicitous, why colours are strong and uncompromising. It also accounts for the subjects chosen, the way they are seen, and for their references to the art of the past. For although they did not dream of identifying with the past, as Morris did, they were familiar with it: they saw the history of art with the eye of the professional who has looked long and keenly at the European tradition. They not only knew what they owed it, but viewed it with intimate love and affection. Much of what we see on the walls of Charleston emerges from this contemplation, often in the form of an ironic but appreciative commentary on some of the artists they most admired.

One of the most interesting aspects of Charleston is this familiarity with a rich cultural tradition, combined with an awareness of the passage of time which belongs to the twentieth century. Charleston is not only a fountain of vitality, springing from the earth of sleepy Sussex, but a protest against an excessively self-conscious desire for permanence and monumentality. In spite of its do-it-yourself air of holiday art – what Phillip Stevens calls 'fun art' – it is a perfectly serious statement that art need not be sententious, that we have reached an age when ephemerality is a more accurate expression of modern life than the longing for the appreciation of posterity. The beliefs of the Victorians were revealed as rather ridiculous, and the excitements of the present moment as spiritually, if not materially, more rewarding.

Nothing at Charleston was treasured for its material value and, until one or two of the paintings were discovered to be worth far more than had ever been imagined, which was not until the late Fifties, thoughts of this nature appear entirely irrelevant. Duncan cherished anything that referred to Vanessa, while she treasured those things painted by him. Some things were more loved than others, and it is typical of their attitude that, when Clive sold his Vlaminck, Vanessa's reaction was to copy it before it left the house, and to hang the copy in place of the original, getting a certain pleasure from contemplating her skill as a copyist, even though it could never be the same. All the things they had picked up abroad in rag markets or junk shops were loved, in exactly the same way as everyone loves accumulated souvenirs: partly for themselves and partly for their associations. But they were also played with, rather as children play with toys they may have temporarily forgotten. Every now and then Duncan and Vanessa would be found, covered with dust and cobwebs, moving a pot or a statue so that it could be seen in a new and more favourable place, or in conjunction with some new gift or acquisition. Things took on a new appearance, even a new life; placed in front of a mirror one would see them both from the front and the back, reflected against a newly painted wall, and one's old pleasure was enhanced by an appreciation of new possibilities.

Painters to the core, Duncan and Vanessa were primarily interested in appearances. These they found so compelling that they needed nothing else to stimulate their painting; they enjoyed the ambiguity, the constant changes, the unexpected relationships that become apparent if things are looked at for long enough with a sufficiently open mind. It was this that informed their attitude to Charleston as a whole: living there was rather like living on a stage where the set is being constantly changed or modified, and it is this that accounts for the nails that support the curtain rods, or the hundred and one expedients that were used to keep the tables from falling or the chairs from collapsing. As long as anything could perform a role in the general scheme of appearances, it was not discarded, although, in the course of time, it might go through a series of metamorphoses. Of course, this style of living is by no means exclusive to Charleston and its inhabitants; we all make do and mend, and it sometimes leads to the production of such exquisite things as patchwork quilts or rag rugs. But at Charleston practically the sole motivation was to satisfy the eye, and when this was achieved there might well be a move towards the paintbox, and yet another picture started in celebration of the visual effect. But it would be a mistake to suppose that this search for visual satisfaction led to a state of self-conscious exhibitionism. Both Duncan and Vanessa were well aware of the role that chance plays in these things; if they kept their eyes open all the time, if they changed and adjusted things, it was always in relation to what was already there, and it is for this reason that we still feel a sense of unity and wholeness about the house and garden.

One can say that Charleston was more Vanessa's creation than Duncan's, if only because a house is, or was, more likely to be a woman's province, and Vanessa had an exceptional ability to create an easy, happy atmosphere. It was not a question of '*le confort*', but a gift for visual harmony which, by suggesting that the mind was at peace, comforted the body. Given minimum warmth, a cushion or two, a curtain, a shaded light and a bookshelf, what more could you want – except of course an easel, a canvas or a wall to paint on? In the garden, for many years more or less neglected, the same feeling prevailed; here the primary requisites were a terrace to sit on and to suggest, perhaps, the *dolce far niente* of a southern climate, a lawn as a concession to people who like the greenness of grass, a pond for reflections and as many flowers as possible for their colour. Statues, gazebos, fruit trees and the like came afterwards. And indeed most of these things we owe to Duncan (who was more of a plantsman than Vanessa), who longed for the unusual and the exotic, and whose dream, it turned out, was of a slightly different nature. As we know, he dreamed of flamingos, but at no time managed to install at Charleston more than two or three Chinese geese. And this hardly mattered, since he was quite capable of thinking he had seen an albatross fly past the window when it was in fact a sparrow. But it was he who bought and installed the life-size cast of Antinous (now disappeared) and the heads on the wall as well as the more unusual plants. Perhaps it was his childhood in Burma which induced this longing for something reminiscent of a sunnier, more Mediterranean, climate, a more Latin influence. It was, when one comes to think of it, of a totally different nature from Vanessa's vision, which was pragmatic, full of acceptance of things as they were, seeing poetry in domesticity, in daisies, snap-dragons and red hot pokers. If she managed to keep Duncan from going beyond the bounds of possibility, she was also delighted by his fantasy, and finally, for our own pleasure, reconciled both extremes.

HOW IT STRIKES A NEW YORKER

John Russell

ONE OF the more remarkable of recent American phenomena is the popularity of Bloomsbury, and by extension of that the popularity of Charleston. People who thought of Charleston as being in South Carolina are beginning to have quite another idea of geography. There is in fact every reason to believe that Charleston will be to the 1990s what Giverny has been to the 1980s – the place to which the cultivated American most wishes to go.

It is a mysterious business. Giverny has associations with which almost everyone can identify – a body of paintings as familiar as any in the canon of French Impressionism, a pretty garden now approaching something like its original garishness, a house in which Monet talked with Clemenceau and what is probably the most celebrated row of poplars in all France.

The American fondness for Charleston is quite another matter. Rare is the American who knows the work of Vanessa Bell or Duncan Grant at first hand. 'No one' reads Clive Bell. The comings and goings between Woolfs and Keyneses and Charleston cannot be imagined without first-hand experience of the Sussex countryside. As for the house, it would tax Chekhov himself to fix it as it was in its heyday.

It may well tax the Charleston Trust also, as I see it. The life of Charleston, as it lingers with this particular and infrequent visitor, was made up in part of things that can be restored and reconstructed. But it was also made up of the imponderable and the fugitive. How to convey to the paying pilgrim the soundless entrances and exits of Vanessa Bell? The irresistible banter of Clive? Or the way in which Duncan's old bones could throw off the very notion of mortality when the talk caught his imagination?

For Charleston was apart from everything else a house in which very funny things were said, continually and without effort. Ideas carried on like Chinese tumblers. Inhibitions, verbal or other, were outlawed. People were themselves, absolutely and without abridgement. Time was as if elasticized. The visitor felt that he had arrived on what the airlines call an 'open-jaw' ticket. Subjects, once raised, would be discussed until the last word had been said. It was not in the nature of Charleston to leave an idea in mid-air.

As to the manner of the discussion, much could be said and many formulations made. The Strachey ingredient was ever exact, clear and emphatic, with many a sharp tap on the kettledrum when one least expected it. Vanessa Bell's interventions were few, but decisive and much sought after. The fly-away fancy of Duncan Grant sounded like someone playing on a wooden-framed piano very fast indeed and with the left-hand pedal down. The point about these conversations was that they had already lasted many years – twenty, thirty, forty – and that there was no reason to suppose that they would ever come to an end. What was not said on any given day would be said on another. It was not a conversation of egoists, either. If people shone, it was the better to throw others into relief. If they were silent – and sometimes it seemed as if they were silent for hours – there was in their silence an element of expectancy that was active, not passive.

Charleston could, I suppose, be called a closed society, in that intruders were few. Strangers were regarded with a lively curiosity the first time round, but in general the cast of characters was complete, and had been complete for a very long time, and there was no more need to annex new characters than there is to double the *dramatis personae* in *Twelfth Night* or *Athalie*. Thence came the continuity of Charleston – a timelessness that extended as much to hats and deck-chairs as it did to turns of speech and affinities across the English Channel.

It is also relevant to the ancient white magic of Charleston that it never looked in any way self-conscious or 'done up'. It was simply the way it was, without curatorial intrusion. An inspired, life-giving untidiness was the mark of much of the house. (Nowhere, by the way, did people ever lie deeper in armchairs.) What in America is called 'maintenance' came a bad fifth to talking, reading, writing and painting.

Charleston tidied up, painted up, curated up, and dis-damped will be an astonishing thing – an ensemble unique in its kind.

It will not be an empty place, like so many houses in which known people once lived. It will not be a dispiriting place, like the former house of George Bernard Shaw, or a polluted place, like the birthplace of Chopin outside Warsaw, where the little stream that Chopin knew now foams green and purple with industrial waste. It will speak to us in the way that book jackets by Vanessa Bell used to speak to us across a crowded bookshop. But something of the give and take of an altogether exceptional society will be lacking. How lucky we are that so much of it has come down to us at first hand, and in print!

EPILOGUE

A TERRIBLE TRAGEDY IN A DUCKPOND

Virginia Woolf

IN THE summer of 1899 Leslie Stephen and his children spent some seven weeks from early August at Warboys, a fenland village in what was then Huntingdonshire, which had 'few shops, four windmills, and nine public houses'. The Rectory, which they rented, was a large, plain, creeper-covered late Georgian house with extensive grounds, and the young Stephens – Vanessa, Thoby, Virginia and Adrian – amused themselves by moth-hunting, boating, and exploring the surrounding countryside on foot, bicycles and ponycart. Among their visitors was a cousin, Emma Vaughan, who spent some ten days with them and participated in the misadventure which is the subject of the following account. This was written by Virginia in the manner of a provincial reporter, sent to Emma for her comments, and later expanded and augmented by 'A Note of Correction and Addition' which in 1904 she recopied and again sent to Emma, who preserved it together with all her letters from Virginia. These now form part of the Monks House Papers in the University of Sussex Library, with whose permission the manuscript is now published for the first time. (Anne Olivier Bell)

A Terrible Tragedy in a Duckpond
(Extract from the Huntingdonshire Gazette)

A terrible tragedy which had its scene in a duckpond is reported from Warboys. Our special correspondent who was despatched to the village has had unrivalled opportunities for investigating the details as well as the main facts of the disaster, & these we have a melancholy pleasure in laying before our readers.

We will shortly mention the groundwork of facts with which it is necessary for the reader to be acquainted before we proceed to the story itself. Mr Leslie Stephen, then an author as some of our readers may know of repute, is spending his summer holidays at Warboys Rectory, the living being held (as we need not inform such of our readers as attend the orthodox church) by the Rev. Bromley Way. The Rectory is a creeper covered house, dating from the beginning of the century, the chief attraction, or at any rate the chief point of interest now, being the garden & the pond. The pond is long & slightly tortuous in its course; an island covered with trees is at one end – the other is said to have some connection with the cesspool of the establishment. So we were informed by an intelligent domestic, by name Mary Roberts, from whom we obtained the greater part of our information. The pond itself is covered with a thick carpet of duckweed, which, being cleft in two by the passage of a boat, yet manages in a few minutes to weave its carpet afresh. We must next notice the punt, which was found capsized on the following morning, & which we were privileged to examine closely. It is an oblong structure, the inside & seats red, & the two ends being also painted the same colour. This punt has often been used without accident by the family, & it was not therefore considered indiscreet when Mr Adrian Stephen suggested to his cousin Miss Emma St John Vaughan that they should go for a moonlight drift in the evening of the 23rd August. It is supposed that Miss Vaughan readily agreed to the plan, & invited Miss Virginia Stephen to join the party. The details of the story can only be guessed at, but my informant Miss Mary Roberts has supplied me with the outline, & I fill in the consecutive links to the best of my ability. A word is needed to explain the age, sex & number of the deceased. In the first place, as the eldest of the party we must name Miss Emma St John Vaughan; of an old Welsh family, we believe, & connected, as her second name indicates, with the noble family of Bolingbroke. She, the first cousin of the Stephens, was paying them a visit of a week or two. She was, as we are assured by Miss Roberts, a young lady of exceptional charm who played the harmonium of an evening 'like an hangel' as the good creature added with tears in her eyes. Secondly and thirdly Miss Virginia Stephen & Master Adrian Stephen, aged respectively 17 & 15, both of them rather inclined to forget the gravity of circumstances in their own high spirits, 'but kind young people Sir, if they did laugh a little foolishly sometimes'. It must be added that the elder brother & sister, Mr Thoby, & Miss Vanessa Stephen, were away at the time, though expected home on the evening of the 23rd.

At about 9.30 then the three stepped into the punt. They had placed in it, with some difficulty, three chairs (in what manner these were found, I shall have occasion to describe)&, seated on these, they pushed off from the bank, & their feet touched land for the last time. It is said that sounds of merriment & song reached the servants as they sat over their supper. 'Ah, there's Master Adrian again,' they said. 'What a noise he do make, to be sure.' It was a bright moonlight night, though half the water was black in the deep shade of the trees. The wind was low, so that it is thought that the sounds (for sounds we fear there must have been) did not carry as far as the house. Mary Roberts informs us that at supper she thought she heard a scream, but when she told the Cook, that authority remarked ''Owever some people can't tell a dog snoring when they 'ears him, surpasses me. Do 'old your tongue, you silly old Mary.' Thus admonished, Mary devoured her pork, & nothing more was said or thought of the mythical screams.

Meanwhile, what a scene was being enacted on the pond! It must be conjectured that the punt was made top heavy by the three chairs which we have already mentioned, & that an incautious movement on the part of one of the crew made the whole thing capsize with deadly swiftness & sureness. Let us picture to ourselves the scene. The three young people were laughing & joking together with infantine light heartedness; the chilly night air served only to brace their spirits; the moon shone calm & benificent; everything even the flat fields & the old white pony were beautiful in her gaze. Suddenly but noiselessly the boat leant to one side, & failed to right itself; the waters rose & rose, irresistible & calm. One moment dry & vigorous, then thrown from the warmth & animation of life to the cold jaws of a sudden & unthought of death – what change could be more absolute or more dreadful? Alone, untended, unwept, with no hand to soothe their last agonies, they were whelmed in the waters of the duckpond, shrouded in the green weed (we believe it to be a species of *Anseria Slimatica*) which we have mentioned above. Thus much we may affirm, but the exact manner & incidents of their deaths must be supplied by each of us according to the fervency of our imaginations. By this time, it being 10 o'clock, Miss Vanessa Stephen & Mr J.T.

Stephen were returned to the house. A short interval passed in which the travellers took off their wraps, before it occurred to them to ask for their guest & their brother & sister. They were probably somewhere in the garden, Mr Stephen answered, & thinking that they had not probably heard the wheels of the carriage which brought the travellers home, the whole party went into the garden to look for them. They called them by name, gently at first so as not to disturb the villagers round, whose rural habits might be supposed to take them to bed before this hour, & to implant in them a puritanical dislike to raised voices after sunset (particularly when such voices issued from the Vicarage) as savouring of drink or perhaps of cards. But as no answer was returned they shouted louder, & a more anxious tone was heard in their voices. Perhaps some bird was roused from its nest & fluttered chirping sleepily through the trees. But there was no sound of answer, or sign of life. The servants were called, & with lanterns they searched every pathway & outhouse. Our informant Miss Roberts states that she bore a candle which she protected by a cabbage leaf, plucked in passing through the kitchen garden. She deposes that when they reached the pond three white birds of great size, as large as swans, & uttering unearthly croaks, rose from the water, &, wheeling round for a time, disappeared into darkness. This was felt to be such a bad omen that as she says, no hope was felt from that moment. Indeed the night grew damp, & the servants crowded together fearful of any object which the rays of their lanterns might disclose. Fairy & Keen, the grooms of the establishment, proved more efficient. The sight of the overturned punt helped them to the decision that the accident was most probably connected with the pond. Fairy, with a heroism that we hope will be rewarded, embarked in an ominous looking square barge, which though half full of rain water & mud was the only craft that remained.

Lighted by the flame of a stable lantern (of which we wished to make a reproduction, but the said lantern being in use at the time we were obliged to refrain) he paddled bravely to the object which he concluded to be an overturned punt. His suspicion proved only too correct; it *was* a punt – *the* punt (no other being possessed by the Rev. Bromley Way) & moreover it was capsized. Floating near by, Mr Fairy found a grey felt hat, a piece of linoleum & a baler, which had in some way escaped filling with water & was floating with the other relics. These touching articles were placed on board the barge – but *nothing else*. The bereaved remnant of the family of Stephen, unable to bear, it is supposed, the terrible suspense of the proceedings, had left the shore, & were giving vent to their grief indoors. It was now close on midnight, & but one conclusion could be drawn; the argument may be roughly set down thus. It is clear from the nature of the articles found in the Punt (felt hat &c) that certain persons were embarked in the Punt; three people are at the present moment missing – Miss Emma St John Vaughan, Miss Virginia Stephen, & Master Adrian Stephen. The punt is found overturned – the three persons mentioned are not found in any condition whatsoever. On these premises we must reluctantly infer that the three persons named were drowned in the duckpond, the punt having been overturned, & the said persons having been satisfactorily proved to have occupied seats in that punt. Operations were at any rate suspended upon this hypothesis. Next morning, I am informed by Miss Roberts, Mr Stephen (the son presumably) was early at work attempting to right the punt, & soon he was joined by others who opened the distressing task of searching for the bodies. The green carpet had closed over its prey: the pond was as unruffled as though no human bodies rested in its maw. Only one discovery of any interest was made, when with great difficulty the vessel was righted. Then were found, fixed firmly to the bulwarks – three chairs – the last seats on earth or water of the doomed young people whose last hours it has been our melancholy duty to record. It is believed that there is a deep layer of mud at the bottom of the pond, & in all likelihood the bodies propelled with all vehemence from the punt are at the present moment firmly imbedded in the clay. A steel coat button has come on shore which we believe adorned the jacket of the ill fated Miss Emma St John Vaughan. But what avail these traces & tidings of the dead, when those who owned them can no longer claim them?

The inquest, we are told by Dr Middlebrooke (Coroner for the Northern division of the County of Huntingdon) must be deferred till the bodies are recovered; at the inquest we will resume & conclude our melancholy narrative.

A Note of Correction & Addition to the above by one of the Drowned

The reporter from the Huntingdonshire Gazette seems to have been a gentleman of considerable imagination. The excellent Mary also can hardly be described as a trustworthy informant, & among her numerous good qualities the intellectual faculties are not pre-eminent. One accurate piece of information however she has somehow blundered into retailing, viz. that the bodies have not yet been recovered. When the 'three white birds almost as big as swans' &c (which our feeble pen is unable to transform into anything more remarkable than the three white ducks which have unfortunately given their name to the pond) disappeared, it will be remembered that the whole body of servants took flight for the kitchen. The corpses, however, emerged from their watery grave, & the corpse who writes this note can testify that her first impulse when she reached the shore was to sink upon its muddy bosom & shriek with – we regret to spoil the picturesque story with such a word – but her shriek distinctly resembled that of a person whose sense of humour is unimpaired by drowning or duckweed.

Far be it from me, however, to declare that the experience appealed entirely to the sense of humour; on the contrary we each felt vividly that other senses go to complete the number allotted us. Fear – craven fear – must be recognised; & my analysis of my sensations proves this ingredient to have been a powerful one. I will try to write briefly, concisely & with no sentimental enlargements, the history of that night as it appeared to me, & I will hint as well as I can, though I shall always be liable to correction, the sensations & experiences of my companions. As the Reporter poetically remarks, sounds of merriment were heard vaguely in the kitchen; truth to tell the party of the punt was an uproarious one. We were all perched on high garden chairs, which gave us a commanding view over the water, & at the same time lent an impetus to any movement that we made. St John sat at one end; my self in the middle, & the Loquacious One at the other end. Our wit flowed freely; I remember that at one period of the evening I was singing loudly with a slight disregard for tune 'Oh Perfect love, all human thought transcending'. The Loquacious One had compiled a grand junction of his three famous & original lines, set to music of his own composition also; St John was proclaiming against the profanity of my choice of a tune, & refusing to help me out with either words or music, at the same time shrieking with laughter & expostulating at the terrible discords which were arising from the Loquacious One's end of the boat. Altogether Mary & the Reporter put the state of things mildly & with a commendable regard for truth, when they stated that 'sounds of merriment' &c. We had reached that state of mind when the most ordinary remark has something of divine wit in it. I remember that the Loquacious One had, in a culminating frenzy of genius, transposed the letters of 'Greedy Pig' (applicable to both his cousin & his sister, I think) so as to form 'Peedy Grig'. Also I remember that I shouted with all the power of my lungs 'Can you swim, St John?' And St John with a happy disregard for the seriousness of her admission, had answered that she 'had never swum a stroke in her life'. Of course this announcement delighted us, & we shrieked all the louder. Then for some reason we wished to row further on, & as there were only two oars, St John seized a baler & scooped pailfuls of water over those who had oars, pretending that in doing so she was helping our progress. We expostulated feebly – & then – slowly the boat leant to one side – I remember wondering in a dazed kind of way when it was going to right itself – slowly the water rose, slowly it trickled over the side – there was a splash – I felt myself thrown into something ice cold. I sank & sank & sank, the water creeping into ears mouth & nose, till I felt it close over my head. This, methinks, is drowning, I said to myself. It seemed an age passed under water in which I realised with a completeness that I have not yet forgotten, that I did not wish to die & that die I would not. *Drowned in a Duckpond*, hammered a persistent base in my head; also a kind of patchwork of insignificant hopes & quarrels of yesterday, insignificant & yet of such pathos that I could have wept – had I not been too wet already. If I had known I was to die, I reflected, I should have made better use of my time than this. But surely all my interests & hopes & fears, so small individually but in their sum making up so vivid a current of life cannot be cast into eternal silence & darkness by an accident so unlooked for & unnecessary. Thus blunderingly I strive to follow out in pen & ink the sensations that were pressed each vivid & lasting in its impression into the space of 3 seconds or so. The next thing I know is that I had fought my mouth & eyes clear of the water, & could breathe again, & I realised that just beside me substantial to the touch was the upturned bottom of the punt. Then the circumstances of the accident which had been blotted out of my mind while I strove under the water, came back to me. I looked round for my companions & saw, a few yards in front of me, the obscure form of St John, who seemed to be almost immersed in the water, as if she were staggering forwards on her hands & knees; each time she emerged I heard her gasp & give a kind of shivering groan. I now felt land of some kind beneath my feel, & knew that for me at least the chance of drowning for this night was over. I reached St John, calling loudly for the Loquacious One's help, but he as yet had not emerged from his temporary silence & retirement. St John gripped my arm, & shivering & gasping we struggled on towards the bank. The Loquacious One by this time rejoined us, & I with great volubility & vehemence expressed my sense of his conduct in upsetting the boat. I must add though that the honour of this feat has been disputed since by St John, who asserts that her performances with the baler gave the final touch to our glorious career. We reached the bank, & suddenly the intense comedy of the whole thing flashed over us. Was it not ludicrous to imagine three sane individuals plunging about in a duckpond in their evening clothes, thinking themselves in imminent risk of drowning? We stopped dead, & yelled, shouted, screamed, with laughter. The Loquacious One had crawled out of the water & was in the act of pulling St John up the bank, which was steep & sticky with mud. I gave two or three attempts to scale the bank, & then gave it up as a bad job & sat down contentedly in the pond. When our first ecstasies of laughter were over we realised that a peculiar biting cold was numbing our limbs; elements of prudence implanted in St John's mind by a vigorous elder sister, now bore a somewhat belated fruits & drove her to insist with unsteady firmness that we should jump up & run as quick as possible to the house. We ran, therefore, holding hands & breaking out into fresh spasms of laughter as we ran. Our clothes flapped round us, but the movement produced a delicious creeping feeling of heat, which began halfway up our legs & crept higher & higher till our whole person was enkindled in its embrace.

For some reason I thought it best that we should make straight for the kitchen, having a vague notion that we should unrobe there & stand nude in front of the grate. We rapped at the kitchen window where the servants sat comfortably over their needlework, & confusedly explained to Sophia who came running out with a startled expression what had happened to us. We got in & ran up the back stairs to our bedrooms; streams of brown water oozed off & marked our passage over the clean white boards. The excellent Mary rose equal to the occasion & after a few 'Ohs!' of astonishment, provided us with hot water, towels, & dry clothes, all badly needed. My own experience was that after I had cast off all clothing, my skin was wet as though I had been bathing, & my hair & body were covered with innumerable bits of duckweed. At this moment the two elders arrived. 'Where *are* the others, Rose?' 'The young ladies & Master Adrian have all just tumbled into the pond, Miss,' said Rose grimly. I shall never forget Nessa's face of shocked dismay when she beheld her family. 'See what happens when I leave you to yourselves,' she repeated over & over again. 'Oh what lunatics – what babes-in-arms – Oh St John how could you?' She was almost inarticulate with the multiplicity of her emotions & the natural difficulty of expressing them all at the same time. St John & I met half an hour afterwards in a costume which under other circumstances we should hardly have worn in public. In the excitement of the moment however we did not precisely consider the relations of bodices & skirts but took what happened to be dry & available. The remainder of that night is vivid in my mind but more like a scene out of a pantomime than a sane Wednesday evening.

Methinks the human method of expression by sound of tongue is very elementary, & ought to be substituted for some ingenious invention which should be able to give vent to at least six *coherent* sentences at once. Then perhaps we should sooner have exhausted the thrilling & mysterious tale of our capsizement. As it is I see no chance that the theme with all its infinite variations & motives & sub-motives, will ever become translated to the world. St John, happy creature, has a piano to speak for her with its variety of voices; but even that fails completely to carry forth the flood. Strangely enough those who happened to be at Gunby that night showed very little sympathy with us or desire to listen to our adventures. But I can affirm I think with some decision, that the analysis of our sensations – how we felt under the water – how we felt when we came to the top, what we saw – how we scrambled out – how we sat on the bank & laughed – &c &c &c will for us at any rate never lose its excitement & charm.

CONTRIBUTORS

NOËL ANNAN is the author of a biography of Leslie Stephen, Virginia Woolf's father. Sometime Vice-Chancellor of the University ofLondon, earlier Provost of King's College, Cambridge.

ALAN BELL is Librarian of Rhodes House Library, Oxford. He edited *Sir Leslie Stephen's Mausoleum Book* for the Oxford University Press (1977), and is interested in the history of the *Dictionary of National Biography*.

ANNE OLIVIER BELL, a student of the Courtauld Institute, worked for the Ministry of Information, the Control Commission for Germany and the Arts Council until her marriage in 1952 to Quentin Bell. Three children. Editor, *The Diary of Virginia Woolf* (five volumes, 1977–84). Committee member of the Charleston Trust since its inception.

QUENTIN BELL, ceramic artist and writer, younger son of Clive and Vanessa Bell, Emeritus Professor of the History and Theory of Art, Sussex University. His books include *On Human Finery* (1947), *Ruskin* (1963), *Bloomsbury* (1968) and *Virginia Woolf: A Biography* (1972). Chairman of the Charleston Trust 1979–86, since then an Hon. Life President.

ASA BRIGGS was Provost of Worcester College, Oxford, from 1976 to 1991 and previously Vice-Chancellor of the University of Sussex. He is a social historian and is President of the Social History Society. He is also a Fellow of the British and American Academies. His books include *A Social History of England* and *Victorian Things*.

ASYA CHORLEY is a Director of the Impressionist and Modern Art Department, Sotheby's, London. After working at the Theatre Museum, London, she joined Sotheby's in 1980, where she trained as an expert in ballet and theatre material. In 1988 she assumed responsibility for sales of Impressionist and Modern drawings and water-colours.

JUDITH COLLINS is Curator of the Modern collection at the Tate Gallery and oversees and cares for twentieth-century British art.

PAMELA DIAMAND, who died in 1985, was the daughter of Roger Fry.

MARTIN GAYFORD was educated at Cambridge and London universities. He contributes regularly to the *Daily Telegraph*, the *Sunday Telegraph, The Spectator* and *Modern Painters*. On occasion he has been known to broadcast. At present he lives in Cambridge with his wife Josephine, small daughter Cecily and infant son Tom.

LAWRENCE GOWING, who died in 1991, was a painter and a writer on painting. He was Slade Professor of Fine Art and Hon. Curator of the Royal Academy collections.

MARGARET DRABBLE is a novelist and critic, author of twelve novels and editor of the fifth edition of *The Oxford Companion to English Literature* (1985). Her most recent novel is *The Gates of Ivory* (1991). She is working on a biography of Angus Wilson.

LEON EDEL is the author of *Henry James – A Life, Bloomsbury, A House of Lions* and other biographical works.

JANE EMERY, of Stanford University, received a Ph.D. in English Language and Literature at the University of Chicago, was granted a Leverhulme Fellowship at the School of English and American Literature at the University of East Anglia and then became a Senior Lecturer at the University of Queensland. After her retirement in 1982 she became a Visiting Scholar at Stanford's Centre for Research on Women and in its English Department, where she now teaches. In 1975, as Jane Novak, she published *The Razor Edge of Balance: A Study of Virginia Woolf* (University of Miami Press). *Rose Macaulay: A Writer's Life*, from which the present essay was adapted, was published by John Murray in 1991.

PENELOPE FITZGERALD is a biographer and novelist who was awarded the Booker Prize for fiction in 1979, and has published the biography of her father and her three uncles, *The Knox Brothers*. She has three children, an economist, a Spanish teacher and a research physiologist, and lives in north London.

ANGELICA GARNETT (née BELL) is the daughter of Vanessa Bell and Duncan Grant. After three years at the London Theatre Studio she 'chose' to be a painter but, seized by biological and other forces, got married to David Garnett and had four daughters. Hypnotized probably by the achievements of her parents, and the memory of the artistic atmosphere at Charleston, she continued to paint. Recently she discovered herself to be more interested in three-dimensional expression, and now makes a kind of sculpture which, depending on materials of almost any description and of the most ordinary nature, also often refers to her continuing love of the theatre. In 1983 she published a short account of her childhood and relationship with her family, *Deceived with Kindness*. She now lives and works in France.

LYNDALL GORDON was born in Cape Town and now teaches in Oxford. She has written three prize-winning biographies, including *Virginia Woolf: A Writer's Life*. Her most recent book is *Shared Lives*.

MITCHELL A. LEASKA is Professor of Humanities at New York University and literary consultant for the *Psychoanalytic Review*. He is author of *The Novels of Virginia Woolf*, editor of *A Passionate Apprentice: The Early Novels of Virginia Woolf* and *The Virginia Woolf Reader*, and co-editor of *The Letters of Vita Sackville-West to Virginia Woolf*. He is director of the NYU Humanities Summer Abroad Program in Greece.

JAMES MACGIBBON published the collected writings of Desmond MacCarthy, critic and friend of Bloomsbury. He came to know Adrian Stephen when they were both in the Army in World War II.

VIRGINIA NICHOLSON is a granddaughter of Clive and Vanessa Bell and a daughter of Quentin and Olivier Bell. She worked in the Documentary Department of BBC Television for seven years and is a Council member of the Charleston Trust. She lives about ten miles from Charleston with her husband, the writer William Nicholson, and two small children.

NIGEL NICOLSON is the younger son of Vita Sackville-West and Harold Nicolson. As his mother was Virginia Woolf's most intimate friend of her middle years, he knew her well as a child. In 1975–80 he edited the six volumes of Virginia Woolf's Letters, and wrote about his parents in *Portrait of a Marriage* (1973).

FRANCES PARTRIDGE, born in 1900, lived in three Bloomsbury squares in turn – Bedford, Brunswick and Gordon. On coming down from Cambridge she worked in Birrell and Garnett's bookshop and subsequently as a translator and literary journalist. She married Ralph Partridge (one son), with whom she edited the Greville Memoirs. She has published seven books since the age of seventy.

JOHN RUSSELL, after twenty-eight years as art critic of *The Sunday Times*, moved to New York in 1974 and has recently retired after some years as chief art critic of *The New York Times*. His books include *The Meanings of Modern Art, Seurat, Reading Russell* and *Paris*. He is working on a book on London and a biography of Eugène Delacroix.

RICHARD SHONE is a writer on art who has been associate editor of *The Burlington Magazine* since 1980. His books include *Bloomsbury Portraits* (1976), *Walter Sickert* (1988) and *Sisley* (1992). He knew Duncan Grant well in the last twelve years of the artist's life and was a frequent visitor to Charleston.

ROBERT SKIDELSKY is Professor of Political Economy at Warwick University and a biographer, notably, of John Maynard Keynes. He has been Chairman of the Charleston Trust since 1987.

SYLVIA STEVENSON is a lecturer and supervisor in the History of Art faculty at Cambridge University and lectures also for the Christie's Fine Art course.

JACKY THOMPSON is a housewife and part-time farmer and teacher of English literature. She is currently working on an essay on Shakespeare and syphilis.

THE CHARLESTON TRUST

THE CHARLESTON TRUST was set up in 1980 to purchase from the Firle Estate, restore and preserve Charleston Farmhouse, in Sussex; and to promote knowledge of Charleston and its historical, literary and artistic connections.

In 1916 Virginia Woolf wrote to her sister, the painter Vanessa Bell, suggesting that she move to Charleston. Vanessa arrived in October with her two sons and the painter Duncan Grant and writer David Garnett. Charleston soon became a focus for writers and painters of the Bloomsbury circle: Clive Bell, Roger Fry, Maynard Keynes, Lytton Strachey and the Desmond MacCarthys were frequent visitors.

Until Duncan Grant's death in 1978 Charleston was a place of continuing creative activity. It offers the only surviving example of the domestic decorative art of Vanessa Bell and Duncan Grant and stands as a monument to a way of life.

Restoration was far enough advanced in 1986 for Charleston to be opened to the public. The Charleston Trust (Charleston Farmhouse, Firle, Lewes, East Sussex BN8 6LL), an independent registered charity, must rely on donations to complete restoration, ensure conservation and maintain the collection.

Charleston is now open to the public on Wednesday, Thursday, Saturday, Sunday and Bank Holiday Monday afternoons, 2 p.m. – 6 p.m., April to October.

The Trust publishes the twice-yearly *Charleston Magazine*, holds an annual festival and presents a variety of applied and fine art in its shop and gallery.

The membership, the 'Friends of Charleston', are entitled to free admission, special openings, private view invitations, the *Charleston Magazine* and other benefits. In America a sister body has been set up, The Charleston Trust USA (Regency House, 221 West 48th Street Suite 1901, Kansas City, Missouri 64112).